Rustproof Relationships Revisited

A Guide to Personal Growth and Achieving Your Dreams and Goals

Diana F. Lee, M.Ed., M.P.A., PMC Transforming Spirituality
Author of:

Rustproof Relationships: A Guide to Healthy Relationships and Effective Communication Skills

Touching the Soul: A Therapeutic Guide to Spiritual and Personal Growth

Therapy Dogs and the Stories They Tell

Rustproof Relationships Revisited

A Guide to Personal Growth and Achieving Your Dreams and Goals

**Diana F. Lee, M.Ed., M.P.A.,
PMC Transforming Spirituality**

Edited by Stanley D. Wilson, Ph.D.

ISBN: 146645492X
ISBN 13: 9781466454927
Library of Congress Control Number: 2011919205
CreateSpace Independent Publishing Platform
North Charleston, South Carolina

One speck of dust contains the
Whole earth;
When one flower opens,
The whole world comes into being.
—Unknown

Acknowledgments

The hardest part of writing this book was finishing it, which took me nearly three years. There are a number of people I would like to thank for assisting in the delivery. Much appreciation to my wonderful editor, Stanley Wilson, Ph.D., a friend who has spent much creative time and effort with me in discussing and honing the ideas I have passed along to my readers. I'd also like to mention Lee Nye, Ph.D.; the Rev. Linda Kaufman, MBA, MDiv, PMC Transforming Spirituality, B.C.C; Sue Keacher, M.Ed.; Kathryn Anderson; Andrea Adams, D.N.; Steve Olsen, N.D.; Anthony Zecca; Sarah Burchfield; Darrell Lee, M.Ed.; William Taylor (beloved husband); and Katherine Lee Taylor (beloved daughter), all of whom have spent time and energy giving me feedback on my raw manuscript. Many of my clients have made positive suggestions on the information that now appears in this book and have thus contributed to its development. A special acknowledgment is reserved for Angela Chase, who has been dedicated to this project and made a number of creative contributions.

Dedication

To my many mentors who have shared their wisdom and guidance with me. Also to those teachers and friends who have helped me along the way—especially Marilyn Conaway (teacher at Bothell High School), Katherine Nelson, M.D., Jess Roebuck, M.D., Judge John Lawson, Professor of Community Service Naomi Goodard (Seattle University), Professor of Art Merdeces Hensley (University of Washington), and Professor of Theology Valerie Lesniak (Seattle University).

Introduction

In this second volume, my focus turns to personal growth, as well as reaching your dreams and goals.

People are hurting and stuck. They struggle unsuccessfully with difficult thoughts, painful emotions, traumatic memories, and failed dreams and goals. I wrote this book because I used to be one of those people. I was so caught up in life's struggles that I questioned whether I could go on. My job was unfulfilling, and I felt trapped in an endless pattern of addictive and abusive relationships. I felt stupid and inadequate, unable to turn my life around.

I decided to do something different—I would learn new skills and new ways of thinking and relating. I made a conscious choice to acquire the skills that would equip me for real and lasting change. Along the way, I discovered that coping skills are the tools necessary for handling the stresses of modern life.

Forty years of successful teaching in my counseling profession has shown me I could educate others about what I'd learned.

For the last fourteen years, I have used three therapy dogs (Brussels Griffons) in my practice. I have used Dr. Jerry, Jack, and Jenny to teach boundary skills along with many of the other skills included in this book. Once clients were taught how to cope, they could tap into their native intelligence, develop their creativity, achieve their goals, and navigate life's ups and downs without falling apart during the tough times.

In the first volume, *Rustproof Relationships: A Guide to Healthy Relationships and Effective Coping Skills* teaches the skills imparted by effective counselors and psychotherapists. These skills should have been taught in childhood but weren't because parents never learned or mastered them themselves. People who lack coping skills are infinitely more vulnerable and less happy. During tough times, their lives spin out of control and they suffer negative thoughts and emotions, such as chronic depression and worry. Worse yet, they relate unskillfully and end up frustrated and lonely, unable to secure the love they need. This book is about how to move from feeling overwhelmed and inadequate to living life to its fullest potential, including healthy self-management and achieving dreams and goals.

On Using This Book

This workbook contains stories and examples that make up a primer for essential coping skills. Clear directions and easy-to-follow worksheets make the process of change a positive experience. Each chapter builds self-awareness and a new perspective that gives birth to a choice: continue to struggle through life with insufficient coping skills or succeed by taking the suggestions placed throughout this book.

To get the most out of your reading experience, do one chapter at a time and participate in all the exercises. Find a safe and comfortable place to do the exercises free from distractions. Be bare bones honest with yourself and prepare for change.

Part One deals with personal growth. These are important issues, such as lifting depression, cooling the flames of anger, building positive self-esteem, learning to forgive, grieving the lost years, spotting the difference between grieving and whining, managing emotional triggers, and making mistakes skillfully.

Part Two is about reaching dreams and goals. Here, we put an end to procrastination, learn to manage perfectionism, and deal with being overwhelmed. We also learn to keep dreams alive, manage fear, make decisions, handle job stress, and achieve our dreams and goals.

My first book, *Rustproof Relationships: A Guide to Healthy Relationships and Effective Communication Skills*, was also divided into two parts, as follows.

Part One is all about relationship skills, for example, how to recognize a safe person, fixing a "broken picker," sexuality, and intimacy. This part will better equip you with skills that will get you the love you want and deserve.

Part Two teaches communication skills. Here I write about setting limits, praising others effectively, and dealing with annoying people. You will learn to be a more effective listener and connect meaningfully with others.

About the Examples in This Book

None of the examples presented in this book reflect the life experiences of any one individual. Rather, each is a composite formed from the lives of numerous people I have known. By using composites and altering the stories I have heard and experienced, I protect the confidentiality of others. Any resemblance between anyone I have known appearing on the pages of this book and a real person is coincidental.

A note about pronouns—throughout the book, I use "he" or "she" interchangeably to refer to the typical child or adult. Any such reference in the text is equally applicable to either gender. Using the more modern and generic "he/she" feels unnatural to the flow of thought. Hence the reader may assume that, unless otherwise stated, any reference to one gender also holds true for the other. Having stated that, most of the examples concern women, as this book is intended primarily for women. However, men will find this book useful as well.

Table of Contents

Poem   vii
Acknowledgments   ix
Dedication   xi
Introduction   xiii
On Using This Book   xv
About the Examples in This Book   xvii

Part One: PERSONAL GROWTH   1

Poem   3
1.   The Balance Beam Is Four Inches Wide   5
2.   Self-Care or Self-Sabotage—Choose Wisely   7
3.   How Do You Know You Are Operating in Reality?   9
4.   Getting Unstuck   15
5.   Grow or Die   25
6.   Anger—A Gift of Energy   33
7.   Beneath the Surface of Anger   39
8.   Protect Yourself and Let Go of Your Anger   45
9.   The Art of Waiting   51
10. Managing Depression (A Step in the Right Direction)   55
11. One Is the Loneliest Number— Celebrating Alone Time   67
12. Sleep Hygiene   71
13 Recharging (You and the Energizer Bunny)   77
14. Working through Grief and Loss   83
15. Grieving the Lost Years   89
16. Looking for the Gifts and Opportunities   97
17. Processing Grief Versus Whining   101
18. About Forgiveness   105
19. Sticky Self-Esteem   109

20. Self-Talk   117
21. Reframing   123
22. Don't Lose Yourself in the "Theys"   129
23. Never Be a Victim Again   137
24. Checking in with Yourself (Managing Emotional Triggers)   143
25. The Difference between Intuition and Triggering   151
26. Probing Your Intuition   157
27. Do Your Passions Match Up with Your Personal Values?   161
28. Me…and My Shadow (Who Is the Observer?)   167
29. Are You Grounded?   171
30. Numbing Out   177
31. Selfish, Selfless, and Self-Caring   183
32. Green Is Good (Turning Jealousy into a Positive)   187
33. Fear Is No Burden   193
34. Making Mistakes Skillfully   201
35. Mom's Comfort List (When Away from Home)   207
36. A More Satisfying Life   211
37. Developing Resilience   215
38. Humor Is a Necessity   221
39. Mindfulness   223
40. Seed an Epiphany   227
41. Something to Fall Back On   231
Poem   234

Part Two: REACHING YOUR DREAMS AND GOALS   **235**

Poem   237
42. Put an End to Procrastination   239
43. Is Being Late a Problem?   247
44. Scattered or Overwhelmed?   255
45. Why Delegate?   261
46. Taking On Too Much (Prescription for Burnout)   `265
47. Collecting Information Based on Reality   269
48. An Unfair World (The Dragonfly Story)   273

49. Can Humility and Confidence Exist Simultaneously?   275
50. Keep Your Dreams Alive   279
51. Achieving Goals—The Art of Calculated Risk   283
52. Decision-Making 1 + 2 = 3   293
53. The Curse of Perfectionism   305
54. Handling Stress on the Job   309

Poem   **316**
About the Author   **319**
About the Dogs   **321**

Part One
PERSONAL GROWTH

Until one is committed, there is hesitancy, the chance to draw back, always ineffectiveness. Concerning all acts of initiative (and creation), there is one elementary truth the ignorance of which kills countless ideas and splendid plans: that the moment one definitely commits oneself, the providence moves too. A whole stream of events issues from the decision, raising in one's favor all manner of unforeseen incidents, meetings and material assistance, which no man could have dreamt would have come his way. I learned a deep respect for one of Goethe's couplets:

Whatever you can do or dream you can, begin it.
Boldness has genius, power and magic in it!'
—W.H. Murray

1
The Balance Beam Is
Four Inches Wide

Life is like riding a bicycle. To keep your balance you must keep moving.
—Albert Einstein

Equilibrium is being in disequilibrium but trusting yourself to come back to balance.

—Phillip Moffitt

Not long before the great psychoanalyst Sigmund Freud died, he was asked the following question: "You've written nearly forty books on mental illness; what is mental health?" Without hesitation, he answered, "Mental health is the ability to balance work, love, and play."

This simple definition is profound yet elusive because of the difficulty in finding the right balance between the conflicting demands of career and family. Recently, I counseled a woman, Rebekka, who lived in Seattle but commuted to Olympia daily, a distance of over fifty miles and more often than not, a two-hour drive in horrid traffic. The woman had a husband and a young son at home, both of whom felt neglected as a result of her ten- to twelve-hour workdays.

Rather than label her a workaholic or lecture her about the lack of balance in her life, I asked Rebekka to do the following exercise. Draw a circle like a big pie, and make it show three slices—one for work, one for love, and one for play. Be sure to make the size of each slice proportional to the percentage of your life taken up by each of the three categories. She drew a pie with a work slice that took up about 90 percent, a love slice that was about 8 percent, and a play slice that was a sliver at 2 percent. I asked, "What did you learn from this exercise?" Her answer was, "I'm like a tire on a car that's out-of-round. I have to change my life to get back in balance."

Of course, I supported Rebekka and also reminded her that on our deathbeds, we are not likely to lament that we didn't work enough. More likely, we would wish we had spent quality time with those we loved and played enough to make ourselves happy. In the space of a few months, Rebekka found a new job only ten minutes from home. Her stress level went way down as her tire came back into round. Events that used to flummox her are currently met with a greater sense of equanimity and sometimes even a chuckle.

It's not about affecting a perfect balance between work, love, and play but noticing how our pie chart breaks down and adjusting accordingly. Try the pie chart exercise for yourself and see where you stand. Are you working too much or playing too much? Not enough love? Take the appropriate actions to balance your life and watch for big changes.

Remember also that balance is about noticing how you respond to difficult people and difficult circumstances and doing your very best to cope without coming apart at the seams. Then, when the inevitable disasters happen and life seems to spin out of control—the computer freezes, the shoelace breaks, the traffic snarls when you're already late, the kid gets a nasty cut on the playground—you can and will cope more effectively as a result of living a balanced life.

2
Self-Care or Self-Sabotage—
Choose Wisely

During the Industrial Revolution, disgruntled workers in Holland would destroy machinery by throwing their *sabots* (wooden shoes) into the moving parts, hence the term *saboteur*. Unfortunately, most of us have a saboteur within our personality, a dark part that wants to gum up the works when things go well or are about to. We can't really get rid of this part, so it is in our best interest to keep an eye on it at all times.

Self-sabotage often occurs in the emotionally-charged arena of romance. You meet Paul, a really decent, dependable guy who treats you with the utmost respect. He's gainfully employed and fun to be around and shares some common interests. You're attracted to him, but he's not nearly as exciting as the guy who just broke up with you to reunite with his ex-girlfriend.

After several dates, you begin to focus on Paul's faults, which include bushy eyebrows and a tendency to blush when he meets your friends. You act disinterested in him at an outdoor party hosted by his best friend and forget to return his midweek phone call. You don't hear from him for a while, and when you run into a mutual friend, you learn Paul has begun to date someone else.

A month later, you're kicking yourself because you now realize Paul was a good catch who was genuinely interested in a meaningful relationship. Herein lies the problem: the saboteur doesn't want a meaningful relationship. Either it doesn't feel worthy, it's afraid of getting rejected, it's too pessimistic to give it a chance, or all of the above.

The antidote to the internal saboteur is good self-care. Choosing to take good care of yourself will raise your self-esteem and allow you to feel worthy of the good things that happen in your life. This is a different perspective than that held by popular culture, which views positive self-esteem as a blessing and negative self-esteem as a curse based on what you did or didn't get from your parents. In my view, self-esteem is more of a by-product of the way you live your life in the present—in particular, caring for yourself consciously and lovingly. Then, if you do get rejected, you have good self-esteem to fall back on.

Eliminating the saboteur is well-nigh impossible, but with a commitment to good self-care, it will take up less space in your personality. Here are ten key questions to assess your commitment to self-care:

1. Am I eating properly, or is my eating disordered?
2. Am I getting adequate sleep?
3. Am I exercising regularly (20 minutes minimum every other day)?
4. Am I allowing any physical health/mental health/spiritual health problems to hold me back?
5. Am I taking my medications as prescribed?
6. Am I suffering from addictions (any behavior I can't stop)?
7. Am I managing my finances responsibly?
8. Am I surrounding myself with positive, supportive friends?
9. Am I setting healthy and effective limits at work and with my friends, family, partner, and children?
10. Am I practicing a spiritual or philosophical belief system that nurtures me?

If you answered in the wrong direction to any of the questions, make a wholehearted attempt to take responsibility for the needed changes. If you cannot readily correct the problem on your own, seek help from a qualified professional. You deserve nothing less than excellent self-care, and sometimes that means asking for help. If you have a toothache, you go to the dentist.

Bind the internal saboteur, and set yourself up for success. Leave no room for failure by covering all your bases. When you're working to achieve personal goals and make your dreams come true, you must not allow the saboteur to take control. Your first and foremost commitment is to good self-care.

3
How Do You Know You Are Operating in Reality?

People only see what they are prepared to see.

—Ralph Waldo Emerson

If you live in denial, if you are disconnected from yourself or numbed out, if you are not connected to reality, if you dwell in the past or live in the future, you cannot function effectively. It is easier to live in reality than fantasy. To practice the following suggestions, it is necessary to be in reality. Therefore, to function effectively, you need to:

1. **Be Present.** *Present* means you are in the here and now so you can benefit from your experiences. It means you are aware of what's happening so you can take appropriate action. Being present allows you to express your wants and needs, to plan, to problem-solve, and to protect yourself. Having presence of mind enhances effectiveness both in the workplace and in your private life. As the saying goes, "You must be present to win!"

2. **Claim Power.** *Power* is the ability to get things done in an effective way. It is having the energy and strength of character to exert control and authority over your own life. It is power that allows us to gather ourselves and mobilize in whatever direction is needed for effective functioning.

3. **Protect Yourself.** To *protect* means to keep something of value from being attacked or damaged. Protection is the preservation of what is important to you in the spiritual, emotional, and physical realms. We protect ourselves when we stay attuned to possible dangers and know how to set boundaries. We protect ourselves when we recognize and respond appropriately to mistreatment and abuse.

4. **Plan Effectively.** *Planning* represents steps taken in advance to bring about a particular objective. To have a plan is to anticipate a course of action. This could mean establishing a time table to get your car's oil changed or taking every form of precaution prior to assuming a risk. It defines your future as well as your present well-being. Good planning includes but is not limited to: finances, education, dating, career, health, family, and retirement; in short, it includes just about everything that concerns success and happiness.

5. **Problem-Solve.** In *problem-solving*, you seek to work out the best possible response to difficult situations or issues both temporary and permanent. It is vital to your life's path, as without it, you will be forever caught up in life's perplexities.

6. **Reach Your Potential.** *Potential* means there is something within us that we have yet to bring into being, such as personal power or the capacity to develop a valuable skill. Unrealized, undeveloped potential is at the core of the human experience. It's what being alive is all about! It's what makes us all uniquely different, and we all have it within us. Recognizing our potential will sow the seeds of creativity and accomplishment.

Some years ago, while traveling in Central Mongolia, I stopped with my tour group to photograph a herd of Takis, also known as Asiatic wild horses. Imagine my excitement at the opportunity to take pictures of the only known surviving species of wild horses on planet Earth. Glancing down to adjust a camera setting, I startled at the sight of a white-and-black striped scorpion, six inches in length, stinger coiled and ready to strike! Instinctively, I jumped back, as the venomous arachnid was a mere four inches before me. At once, I alerted my Dutch group guide, who had been standing immediately next to me, very much in harm's way. Despite the fact he was wearing open-toed sandals without socks, he replied somewhat casually, "I'm not going to change my shoes." With some alarm in my voice, I told him he was in danger and I didn't want to be responsible for carrying him back to civilization. He acknowledged the scorpion's presence but to my astonishment, continued photographing and did not move to safety.

A second guide came upon us, a native Mongolian woman, and I urgently pointed out the scorpion to her. She replied, in a mechanical voice, "There are no scorpions in Mongolia."

Pointing to the predator, I asked, "Then what do you call this?"

She replied in the same droning voice, "There are no scorpions in Mongolia," never acknowledging that anything was there!

<u>What just happened, and how does operating in reality apply?</u>

<u>When I am present</u>, I notice the scorpion and my awareness mobilizes me to take appropriate action—namely, to jump back and warn others.

<u>When I own my power</u>, I assert myself by saying what's so. I use my energy to remove myself from a dangerous scorpion.

<u>When I am in a protective</u> mode, I acknowledge reality so I can avoid harm. Unlike the guides in the story, one of whom minimized and one of whom was so in denial she was totally disconnected from reality, I was able to prevent myself from being injured or killed.

<u>When I plan</u>, I take the steps necessary to ensure my survival.

<u>When I problem-solve</u>, I work out an optimal solution to a difficulty. In this case, I removed myself to a safe distance and then warned others.

<u>When I realize my potential</u>, I greet whatever situation I find myself in with every possible resource within me, whether it's already there or not.

It is imperative that you are connected with yourself, grounded in reality, and living in the present. This will allow you to plan, problem-solve, and protect and empower yourself so you can realize your potential. Without operating in reality, it will be extremely difficult to achieve your life's dreams, goals, and ambitions. Your scorpion might be a bad relationship, a toxic job, or a dysfunctional family.

As a side note, the reality is there are three subspecies of scorpions in Mongolia. I did some research. It was just blind luck or the grace of God that no one was stung. The fact remains the venomous scorpion could have killed someone, as proper medical attention would have been impossible because we were geographically isolated.

A great recovery saying is, "Insanity is doing the same thing over and over and expecting a different outcome." In other words, insanity occurs when you operate outside of reality.

When you are operating in reality, you have a sense of centeredness and being grounded. You are more apt to feel calm and trust that you are operating in reality, rather than questioning your perception. The pain of questioning your perception is one of the worst a person can experience. If you cannot trust your perception, then it is very hard to trust the core of yourself, your center, your self-esteem, your value, and your worth.

Here are some good tips for how it feels to experience reality:

When you are around people you respect and trust, you'll find that your perception and theirs are pretty close to the same.

- How are you experiencing reality? When you are experiencing, thinking, feeling, seeing, hearing, sensing, if you feel well-grounded, centered, and calm, more than likely, you are in reality.

When you are not in reality, you might experience:

- Feelings of immaturity
- Feelings of being out of control and accompanying behaviors like swearing
- Depression
- Anxiety
- Obsession/rumination
- Fear

- Feelings of childishness
- Feeling overwhelmed
- Confusion
- Low self-confidence
- Feeling crazy
- Disorientation, spacyness
- Someone telling you that you are "out to lunch"

4
Getting Unstuck

Stuck (stŭk) v. Past tense and past participle of stick. To be at or come to a standstill; become fixed, blocked, checked, or obstructed.
— *The American Heritage Dictionary*

Amy, a bright college graduate in her early twenties, felt paralyzed by indecision. Should she take a job to pay off her fifty thousand dollars in undergraduate loans or return to school and pursue a master's degree? If she did choose to enter graduate school, should she study foreign languages and become an interpreter or get a teaching certificate and become an educator? If she decided to attend school, which program would be right for her? The state college would allow Amy to save money and stay close to home, but the prestigious private school back east would give her better job opportunities once she completed her studies. What if she committed to graduate school only to learn she'd made the wrong choice? The more she ruminated, the more she felt stuck. Feeling stymied and unable to make any choice at all, Amy entered therapy.

If you are unsure where your life is headed, sit with and examine your own stuck points and get moving. Here are the steps I used with Amy to help her move through her impasse:

1. **Name the Issue.** Give the issue a name, and learn the language to describe it. It will help you to talk about it, as it makes it easier to grasp and work with. Amy named her stuck point "Quicksand," which helped her take responsibility for feelings of fear and shame. Once you see the problem and step back from it, you can move toward resolution. "Quicksand" became the problem, not Amy!

This idea, borrowed from Narrative Therapy, takes away the feeling there is something wrong with us.

2. **Explore the Issue.** Be curious about your issue and willing to explore whatever thoughts, feelings, and associations come up when you observe it. Talk about your options, journal your feelings, read up on your various choices, or use any other method that will help you make a decision.

3. **Ask Yourself the Three Questions.** Imagine you've committed to a particular course of action, and ask yourself the following three questions. Will this path: (a) put me in touch with people with whom I feel kinship? (b) represent a good fit with my best strengths and most important values? (c) provide meaning and fulfillment over time?

4. **Get Out a Road Map.** Formulate a strategy to attend to the issue. Write out the steps you will need to take, including what to do, what you need to stop doing, what to do next, and whom to seek for help. This is your road map for the journey.

5. **Call for Assistance.** Seek advice from someone safe who succeeds in the areas under consideration. For Amy, this was a high school principal and a vocational counselor. It could also be a friend, mentor, minister, or personal coach. Spiritual support is also important; this could mean, for example, talking to your Higher Power, consulting a trained Spiritual Director, cultivating an inner guide, or following a philosophical belief system. If you believe in angels, summon them. The important thing when you're stuck is to call for assistance.

6. **Practice Mindfulness.** Notice your stuck point whenever and wherever it comes up. Be mindful, and develop the observer part of yourself that watches your experience. Be aware of what happens

in your body. Do you have sensations of tightness, tense muscles, stomach knots, or headaches? What do these sensations say to you? Give them a voice, and listen to the wisdom of your body. Attend to feelings, such as anger or fear, and remember they are arrows to direct your actions. Do not judge being stuck, or if you do, try to have compassion for yourself.

7. **Accept Your Fears.** Identify any fears that might be holding you back. Many years of experience tells me you are unlikely to work through all the fear and then proceed without fear toward your goals. That's OK. Accept the fear, face it down, and do it anyway. Notice how you frighten yourself with your self-talk. Amy's version was to tell herself, "Whatever I do will be wrong!" This, of course, paralyzed her with fear and indecision. The antidote was to detach from this thought by saying, "My mind is having the thought that whatever I do will be wrong, but it's just a thought." As psychologist Steven Hayes points out, "There is a difference between having a thought and buying into a thought!" Amy also disputes the thought: "There is no factual basis for me to believe whatever I do will be wrong."

8. **Be Patient.** Getting unstuck takes time, as well as effort and aim. Taking small steps ensures success. Breathe during moments of impatience and focus on the big picture. You don't take bread out of the oven just because it's time for dinner. You wait until the bread is baked. This is a hard lesson in an era of instant gratification, but it is one that must be learned to get unstuck. Change takes time. You don't learn to play the cello in a week!

9. **Come to Terms With the Issue.** Feeling stuck can be a manifestation of avoidance. Amy's stuckness had to do with her fear of making mistakes. As a child, her parents were overly critical and she learned a "no mistakes" rule. In counseling, she learned to accept herself as fallible and accept her parents as poorly equipped for parenting in

regards to accepting imperfection. Acceptance is here defined as, "You don't have to like it, but you find a way to live with it." It is an act of surrender.

10. **Flex Your Coping Muscles.** Inflexibility lends itself to staying stuck. In T. S. Eliot's *The Cocktail Party*, one character chastises another by saying, "You're nothing but a set of obsolete responses." If you find yourself unable to respond flexibly to some situation, notice how it happens and consider another way of doing things. Say your primary coping skill is to eat pizza and potato chips when you feel stressed out. Flexibility here would mean being willing to feel your feelings and try coping in a healthier way, such as phoning a friend, exercising, meditating, praying, or all of the above. If you slip and eat a bag of potato chips to avoid feeling anxious, it's part of the process. Learn from the slip, and get back on the wagon.

As you can see, getting unstuck requires accountability. Look for the ruts in your life that stop you from making changes, as well as self-defeating patterns that prevent success. Amy worked these steps and decided to return to school, accepting the idea that she would never have 100 percent certainty this was the absolute best path at this time in her life.

Read the following poem by Portia Nelson, and look for the holes you've fallen into. Be bare-bones honest with yourself, and take responsibility for walking down another street. It's easier in the long run.

Autobiography in Five Short Chapters

1.
I walk down the street.
There is a deep hole in the sidewalk.
I fall in.
I am lost…I am hopeless.
It isn't my fault.
It takes forever to find a way out.

2.

I walk down the same street.
There is a deep hole in the sidewalk.
I pretend I don't see it.
I fall in again.
I can't believe I am in this same place.
But, it isn't my fault.
It still takes a long time to get out.

3.

I walk down the same street.
There is a deep hole in the sidewalk
I see it is there.
I still fall in... it's a habit
My eyes are open
I know where I am
It is my fault.
I get out immediately.

4.

I walk down the same street.
There is a deep hole in the sidewalk
I walk around it.

5.
I walk down another street.

—Portia Nelson

Getting Unstuck Worksheet

1. **Name the Issue:**

   _____

   _____

   _____

2. **Explore the Issue** (journal, read about choices, gather information that will help you make a decision):

   _____

   _____

   _____

3. **Ask Yourself the Three Questions:**

   a. **Will this path put me in touch with people with whom I share a kinship?**

   _____

   _____

   _____

   b. **Will this path represent a good fit with my strengths and values?**

   _____

   _____

   _____

   c. **Will this path provide meaning and fulfillment over time?**

   _____

   _____

   _____

4. Get Out a Road Map (steps you'll need to take and what to stop doing):

_____

_____

_____

5. Call for Assistance (seek safe advice from someone who succeeds in the area):

_____

_____

_____

6. Practice Mindfulness (awareness without judgment):

    a. Where is your stuck point?

_____

_____

_____

    b. What do you notice when you are stuck?

_____

_____

_____

    c. What are your emotional and physical cues?

_____

_____

_____

    d. What do these sensations say to you?

_____

_____

_____

    e. **What can you say to yourself?**

_____

_____

_____

7. **Accept Your Fears:**

    a. **Name the fears:**

_____

_____

_____

    b. **Detach or dispute with self-talk:**

_____

_____

_____

8. **Be Patient:**

    a. **Self-talk:**

_____

_____

_____

    b. **Break the strategy into smaller steps:**

_____

_____

_____

9. **Come to Terms with the Issue** (grieve and find acceptance):

_____

_____

_____

10. Flex Your Coping Muscles (list ruts or self-defeating patterns):

_____

_____

_____

If you will change, everything will change for you. Don't wait for things to change. Change doesn't start out there. Change starts within. And when you change, miraculously, your relationships, your health, your business, your children, EVERYTHING else changes around you. But all change starts with you.

—Jim Kohn

5
Grow or Die

The journey to happiness involves finding the courage to go down into ourselves and take responsibility for what's there: all of it.

—Richard Rohr

Character isn't something you were born with and can't change, like your fingerprints. It's something you weren't born with and must take responsibility for forming.

—Jim Rohn

If you don't accept responsibility for your own actions, then you are forever chained to a position of defense.

—Holly Lisle

Larry, a retired client of mine, reported having made some disparaging comments about a friend named Steve that turned out to be not only false, but damaging to Steve's reputation at the golf club. Larry admitted that he'd based his assertions on a series of wild assumptions that had no merit. Word got back to Steve, who angrily and appropriately demanded an apology by telephone. At this point, Larry defended himself and deflected blame back on Steve for not communicating more clearly. However, Larry knew he was in the wrong and wanted help with the dilemma he'd created first by speaking carelessly and then by compounding his error by not taking responsibility.

I ended up in an emergency meeting with Larry, encouraging him to step up and take responsibility for his gossiping. We discussed the Buddhist concept of "Right Speech," of saying what's so, but doing it mindfully and with loving-kindness. We talked about the choice to grow in response to the emotional crisis he faced or suffer a death of integrity. Over the course of an hour, we came up with some ideas that allowed Larry to own up to what he'd done and become a better man. Here are the steps we followed, pretty much in order:

1. **Admitting.** Begin by admitting you have a problem or that you have behaved badly. Self-awareness is the first step to taking responsibility and correcting a character flaw or a mistake. Larry had already done this by the time he raised the issue with me.

2. **Accepting.** Accept there is a problem not just on a thinking level, but on an emotional one as well. For Larry, this meant letting in the feelings of embarrassment and shame connected with having harmed a friend. It also meant confronting the rigidity of his beliefs and his own intolerance, as his judgments about Steve had to do with religious differences.

3. **Cultivate Spiritual, Religious, or Philosophical Support.** Ask for spiritual, religious, or philosophical support to help you get through. Offer prayers if you're so inclined, and ask for courage, strength, and support. Because Larry was a Christian, he could ask God for help. If you don't have a belief system, seek counseling, see a mentor or anyone who will help your development. Consider cultivating some sort of belief system.

4. **Make Amends.** Make amends or apologies to others if appropriate. Larry phoned Steve and made a sincere apology, admitting that he had wronged him. The basic rule is that the amends will not hurt you or someone else. You can do this in person, over the phone, by letter, through e-mail, or any way that seems appropriate. If the apology would hurt someone else, or might, keep it to yourself. I'll never forget a male client who'd regularly peeped on his stepdaughter when she was in the shower. Against my advice, he told

her and threw her into a crisis as she'd not known of the violation. He did it for his own benefit, not for her. Had she asked him, then it would have been appropriate to tell the truth.

5. **Develop Self-Talk.** Use positive self-talk to change old perceptions and beliefs and add new ways of doing things. Write the positive self-talk down, where it is easily accessible for repetition. This way, you can wire in the new learning. Larry's work went thusly: "I put down religions other than my own. I am certain about things that are uncertain." His new affirmations became: "I will be curious about and respect religions other than Christianity" and "There is no absolute reality. I cannot always be certain!"

6. **Be Aware of Triggers.** Watch for emotional triggers; in other words, notice what situations or circumstances cause the old and unwanted behavior to reoccur. For example, driving past a liquor store may trigger drinking in a recovering alcoholic or having a conversation with a critical parent may trigger shame. For Larry, any discussion about religion triggered him and he had to learn to tolerate different belief systems. It helped when I reminded him that Jesus was Jewish.

7. **Notice Self-Cues.** Attend to cues that tell you you're about to fall into the old behavior or pattern you're trying to change. Examples would be how you feel a surge of energy, a shrinking sensation, tightening in your jaw or your teeth clenching, shoulders tensing, heaviness in your chest, and so on. Imagine you have a built-in observer who is noticing what you're doing, thinking, or feeling (because you do). Turn up the imagined observer knob on high to catch yourself slipping into the unwanted behavior. Larry knew he was about to slip whenever he would fold his arms in response to conversation about religion.

8. **Reflect.** Check in with yourself and think seriously about the changes you desire. Share your observations and process with safe people.

See a counselor if necessary. Use mentors or friends to understand your behavior and why it happens. Keeping a journal is effective in cultivating awareness and ultimately understanding your behavior. Journaling will help you see your repetitive and circular thinking, as well as negative actions and thoughts. If you can't let go of repetitive behavior or negative thoughts, you may need to get an evaluation for counseling or medication management. Larry's reflections led to an appreciation that many religions predated Christianity and may have even influenced Jesus in his teachings.

9. **Create a Plan of Action.** Come up with a plan for changing any unwanted behaviors. Gather information, read books, listen to tapes or CDs, talk to safe people, consult a counselor, or join a growth group. Write out a plan of action to amp up your commitment to change. Include a list of alternative ways to handle the problem situation. Put it where you can read it every day until the changes occur and become second nature (use the following Plan of Action worksheet). Larry read two excellent books on the similarities between Christianity and Buddhism, an exercise that greatly improved his tolerance.

10. **Cultivate Patience.** Develop patience, as it takes time to make personal changes. There are reasons for you being the way you are, and sometimes it's hard to let go of an old behavior because you will feel less secure and more anxious. Moreover, the brain resists change. So be forgiving and gentle with yourself when you repeat the behavior you want to change. Larry found it helpful to remember the *Autobiography in Five Chapters* and the *Serenity Prayer*.

11. **Know What to Do When You Slip.** When you slip, and you likely will, take time to reflect and check in with yourself. Look for the trigger that caused you to fall back into the old pattern or behavior. Identify the stimulus that activated the unwanted response. Take a

deep breath, and collect yourself. Remember you are in a learning *process*. I had Larry remind himself why he wanted to change by listing the negative and oppressive consequences of not changing (e.g., sounding like a bigot, alienating friends, and…not conducting himself like a good Christian!).

12. **Revise the Plan.** Revise the plan as often as you need, and rerevise it until you arrive at the most effective plan for change. On a daily basis, make the plan available for revision and consider any idea that will get you closer to your goal. Just don't take on too many behavioral changes at once, as this could overwhelm you. It could derail you or set you up for failure (an example would be going on a diet while trying to quit smoking during a major life stress). Larry's biggest revision was to decide he could be curious about other religions even if he believed his was best for him. To say, in effect, "I see it differently," rather than "You're wrong!"

Targeted Behavior

Behavior_____

Date of Success:	Date of Slip:	Duration of Slip:
1.	1.	1.
2.	2.	2.
3.	3.	3.
4.	4.	4.
5.	5.	5.
6.	6.	6.

7. _____	7. _____	7. _____
8. _____	8. _____	8. _____
9. _____	9. _____	9. _____
10. _____	10. _____	10. _____
11. _____	11. _____	11. _____
12. _____	12. _____	12. _____
13. _____	13. _____	13. _____
14. _____	14. _____	14. _____
15. _____	15. _____	15. _____

Plan of Action

Behavior Goal: _____

Books, CDs, DVDs, or any information specific to the behavior and dates to do research/read:

1. _____
2. _____
3. _____
4. _____
5. _____
6. _____

Safe people to talk to and dates/times to meet:

1. _____
2. _____

3._____
4._____
5._____
6._____

Counselor or support group and dates/times to meet:

1._____
2._____
3._____
4._____
5._____
6._____

Self-talk:

1._____
2._____
3._____
4._____
5._____
6._____

When the behavior occurs:

1._____
2._____
3._____
4._____
5._____
6._____

Triggers that set behavior off:

1._____
2._____
3._____
4._____

5._____
6._____

Cues, physical/emotional:

1._____
2._____
3._____
4._____
5._____
6._____

Alternative, positive behavior:

1._____
2._____
3._____
4._____
5._____
6._____

Growth

All growth—psychological, moral, spiritual—calls for continual beginning. The life journey constantly defeats a person. The struggle is difficult; the temptation is often to give up or even to end the effort by self-destruction. This temptation may take the form of superficiality, becoming a role, instead of a person, spoliation or literal suicide…

To keep on struggling upward calls for continuing "infancies." The child meets the new moment, the new day, the new experience with a kind of trust, an enthusiasm, which turns each into a "new life."…The child-like Pilgrim…stands for the recurrent need of society to begin again on the spiral of time, to use insight into the past errors, and the glories of history to change history.

—Mary Patricia Sexton, CSJ

6
Anger—A Gift of Energy

Anger is a tool, not a master. It will always tell us that it is time to act in our own best interests.

—Julia Cameron

Anger is the emotion preeminently serviceable for the display of power.
—Walter Bradford Cannon

My years working in probation have shown me some practical ways of dealing with anger and—believe me—those who run afoul of the law carry a lot of rage. In this chapter, I share what I have learned.

Thoughts almost always precede emotions; for example, thoughts of danger generate fear, and thoughts of trespass generate anger. According to this theory, the way we think about and interpret the past has much to do with the intensity of our emotion.

When I first started doing psychotherapy, I encouraged my enraged clients to ventilate, and they were more than glad to comply, pounding pillows and screaming epithets at those who victimized them. But my clients didn't often improve; in fact, they dwelled on their feelings of outrage and sometimes became even angrier.

Now I teach people to change their thinking and detach from intense and vengeful thoughts. And it works. By learning to watch your angry thoughts rather than judge them, analyze them, or act them out, you allow them to dissipate and free yourself up.

Keep in mind that anger is a "God-given emotion" (energy in motion), hardwired in the factory. In and of itself, anger is not destructive, but because we sometimes express our anger in harmful or self-defeating ways, we are tempted to judge anger as bad or terrible. Shame or guilt over anger is only appropriate if we have misused it and hurt another person or ourselves.

Anger is about energy. The next time you're angry, get out of your head and allow yourself to feel it energizing your body. Like an arrow, anger points us in the direction of taking action when we feel mistreated or intruded upon. Anger gives us the power to get things done, set a limit, or problem-solve in difficult circumstances.

Anger has survival value, calling us to our battle stations to meet an annoying intrusion or perceived threat to our safety, whether physical or psychological. It is a positive emotion inasmuch as it tells us when we feel the need to set a limit or prepare a defense. This is healthy anger, enhancing communication while ensuring survival. The following situations are examples of when anger is helpful. Your boyfriend calls you a "selfish bitch," and you tell him he has abused you and the relationship is over. Your neighbor repeatedly allows her poodles to trample your flower beds and poop on your lawn, and you ask her to confine them or risk a report to animal control.

Healthy anger functions like an arrow, directing you to take appropriate actions on your own behalf. Unhealthy or abusive anger stops constructive communication and leads to abuse or violence. Here, anger has metastasized into rage, gotten you in its grip, and convinced you to act out in ways that harm others.

When Lydia, a Native American living on a reservation in poverty, thinks about the land that was illegally taken from her people, she feels bitter hatred toward all whites. On a trip to the outlet mall, she gets in a dispute over a parking place and bloodies the lip of a Caucasian. Her rage from the injustice to her people is just; acting it out is abusive (not to mention illegal).

At one time or another, almost everyone falls victim to someone else's inappropriate expression of anger. It could have been an out-of-control parent, a boss, an older sibling, a boyfriend or girlfriend, or a spouse. As a result, we may equate anger with abuse. This is a mistake.

Anger is a natural human emotion that only becomes a negative when poorly managed. Don't be afraid. Make friends with your anger, and use it to move your life forward. If, however, you find yourself mismanaging your anger and harming yourself or others, here are some strategies to tame the beast:

1. **Take a time-out.** Sometimes our anger feels like it's too much to contain. We feel overwhelmed or enraged, and anger spills over in ways we regret. When your anger is too intense to be used in a positive or productive way, you can take a time-out and follow these suggestions:
   a. Breathe deep into your tummy, and cool down.
   b. Decide *not* to strike while the iron is hot.
   c. Take the one action that will best solve your problem.
   d. Stay focused on what you *can* do, not on how helpless you feel.
   e. Let it go (after acting on or expressing your anger).

2. **Take care of yourself when stressed.** Attend to bodily and emotional cues, as well as thought processes that tell you when you're overloaded. Be aware of stressful environmental factors, such as job demands, too much to do, losses of any kind, deaths, and major life transitions. Develop a routine that works for you to lower stress—savor a cup of herbal tea, enjoy a bubble bath, burn candles, exercise, meditate, pray, read for pleasure, inhabit a quiet space, talk to friends, listen to soothing music, breathe deep down into your tummy, or watch *Seinfeld* reruns and have a good laugh. Experiment and learn your most effective way to lower stress, and then write it down and follow it.

3. **Attend to physical or medical issues.** If you suffer from a chemical imbalance that can affect mood swings (a "no-fault" brain disorder), get medical help with medication, herbal remedies, vitamin therapy, and talk therapy. If you are self-medicating with alcohol, drugs, or food, acknowledge the problem and make a plan to deal with it. Smart people get help!

4. **Change your self-talk.**
   a. "I don't have to take it personally."
   b. "This is not about me."
   c. "This is what I'd expect from a disrespectful teenager."
   d. "I'm taking a time-out before discussing this."
   e. "I choose to turn this over to my Higher Power."
   f. "This is not a good time to deal with this."
   g. "I can let it go."
   h. "It's not worth it."
   i. "I need to stay in my Adult."
   j. "Don't go there now."
   k. "I won't go into my lower self just because he did."
   l. "Watch those judgments!"

5. **Express yourself to others.**
   a. "In the future, if I say 'stop,' I expect you to take that as a cue that I am not willing to continue the conversation until a later date and time."
   b. "This isn't a good time."
   c. "Let's take a time-out and set up another time."
   d. "Let's come back to this after we've cooled down."
   e. "I'm tired, and it has been a bad day. I need to set another time to talk."
   f. "I love you."
   g. "I have feelings, too; let's not hurt each other."
   h. "Let's stick to the issue. We can talk about other issues later."
   i. "Let's not say things we'll be sorry for."
   j. "I disagree, but I'm interested in your opinion."
   k. "Let's agree to disagree about this."

A Chinese proverb teaches us, "If you are patient in one moment of anger, you will escape a hundred days of sorrow." How true! With awareness, we have the choice of giving in to or standing up to anger. When we give in, our anger can become a fire-breathing dragon that damages our relationships and our lives.

By following the strategies in this chapter, you can learn to disengage and use anger constructively. Instead of acting out, you can leave an angry discussion, write an angry letter with no intention of mailing it, or take a brisk walk. The way to tame anger is *not* to strike while the iron is hot but to reengage after collecting yourself. This will make anger a tool, not a master.

7
Beneath the Surface of Anger

Here in the world, anger is never pacified by anger. It is pacified by love. This is the eternal truth.

—Buddha

Between the inevitable stresses of life in general and annoying people in particular, we are often drawn into our lower selves. The lower self, the most reactive part of us, is like a powder keg waiting to explode, and every day, there are sparks. An inattentive and dangerous driver is a spark, a family member who speaks unkind words is a spark, a setback at work is a spark, a child who behaves badly in public is a spark, a jealous and possessive life partner is a spark, harsh criticism or judgment from almost anyone is a spark, the memory of an unresolved traumatic experience is a spark. I could go on and on; there are literally hundreds of situations that can spark us to anger.

Yet, often, when we display anger, it is not our primary feeling. If a friend kicks you hard on the shin, you get angry, but first, it hurts, physically and emotionally. Hurt is the primary emotion, and anger is secondary. It's easier and makes you feel less vulnerable to say, "I'm angry" than "I'm hurt." The hurt remains hidden and often unexpressed. There is a cost if the hurt stays under the surface. The unacknowledged emotion harms you, the other person involved, and the relationship.

Suppose your husband or boyfriend criticizes you for overcooking the turkey he won in the company raffle. He makes an insensitive comment, such as, "It's as dry as a bone." Your most effective communication might be something like, "Ouch, that really hurt. In the future, I'd appreciate it if you'd keep a criticism like that to yourself." Ah, but this isn't easy when you are in the moment and upset that he would talk to you that way. It's hard not to come back with something like, "Cook it yourself next time, you jerk!" Of course, it's better to keep that bullet in the chamber because now things have escalated and it doesn't matter who started it. Nastiness begets nastiness!

This also holds true for fear. Rather than say, "I'm frightened," or "You scared me," we put on a show of anger. Men in our culture are the worst offenders here, but women are not immune. Let's say you're on a ride in the mountains with a friend, and she drives ten miles an hour over the speed limit and makes dangerous passes on a two-lane highway. An oncoming car could veer over the center line, or a deer could bolt out at any moment. Eventually, it is bound to happen; you nearly get into an accident, and you explode, "If you keep driving like a maniac, you're going to get us killed!" It would be better to make the fear primary and say, "Wow, that was close. Please slow down and stop passing. I get really scared." Better yet, do it before you get too frightened or almost get into an accident. This makes the point that feelings are to be used, not gotten rid of or suppressed.

Notice that you are more likely to get what you want when you make the hurt or the fear primary. When we make anger the issue, getting what you want or need is not as likely. This doesn't mean you can't still express your anger, but make it secondary. Using the previous examples, you could tack on a comment such as, "I get angry when you criticize my cooking. Please be more considerate in the future," or "It bothers me that you'd drive like that and scare me out of my wits. I'm asking you not to do it again." In both examples, effective communicators end up by stating clearly what they want. They don't just complain or attack; they make a clear assertion about what they need going forward and how the offender could make amends.

Amanda entered therapy wanting to know if she should stay with her husband of thirty-five years. They were a well-to-do couple who enjoyed boating on the Puget Sound with friends. The problem was that for Amanda and her spouse, boating involved parties with a lot of drinking, and alcohol turned Bob into a cad. After four or five drinks, he would make off-color comments to her female friends and, on occasion, touch them inappropriately. Amanda was furious and understandably so, but her primary feeling was one of embarrassment and humiliation.

Fronting with anger had gotten Amanda nowhere; Bob would yell back or stonewall her with defensiveness. When she realized her primary feeling was shame, she was able to approach him in a different way. She told her husband she was mortified when he talked and acted that way with her female friends. This got through to him, and he acknowledged he had a problem and agreed to enter therapy with a counselor specializing in substance abuse. Note how much easier it is for someone to hear, "I feel so embarrassed when you act that way," as opposed to "You're acting like a creep, and if you don't stop it, I'm going to divorce you." The unconscious shame had to be expressed first.

Ask yourself about the feelings in you that may come before your anger, but remain beneath the surface. Be truly honest with yourself. Put a checkmark next to the number, and then write about these feelings until you become comfortable expressing the primary emotion. Anger is often triggered by, but actually secondary to the primary feeling of:

____ **1. Fear** _____

____ **2. Guilt** _____

____ **3. Humiliation** _____

____ **4. Rejection** _____

____ **5. Hurt** _____

____ **6. Being Discounted** _____

____ **7. Being Ignored** _____

____ **8. Insecurity** _____

____ **9. Not Being Listened To** _____

____ **10. Not Being Good Enough** _____

____ **11. Being Threatened** _____

____ **12. Being Abused** _____

____ **13. Vulnerability** _____

____ **14. Embarrassment** _____

____ **15. Being Unimportant** _____

____ 16. **Being Found Out** _____

____ 17. **Being Out Of Control**_____

____ 18. **Inadequacy** _____

____ 19. **Being Left Out** _____

____ 20. **Sadness** _____

____ 21. **Any Other Feeling(s) That Comes Before Anger** _____

We've been talking about coming out with anger even though some other feeling is primary. But, sometimes, it's the anger that's hidden from consciousness. When anger is secondary to some other emotion, we look deeper for what is primary.

Hidden anger is usually the result of not getting our needs met, suffering an emotional wound, or having someone intrude upon our personal space. At other times, we hide anger for fear of retribution. It's just not safe to express anger.

By hiding anger from ourselves, we betray our inner voice of authenticity. Family-of-origin modeling and culture teach us, especially women, to hide angry feelings, but this hurts us on many levels—personal, physical, emotional, spiritual, and relational.

Below are the fifty most common signs of hidden, unexpressed anger.

Checklist for Hidden Anger

1. ___ Habitual lateness
2. ___ Enjoying biting humor
3. ___ Sarcasm, cynicism, flippant conversation
4. ___ Procrastination in finishing imposed tasks
5. ___ Smiling while hurting inside
6. ___ Over-controlled, monotone voice or loud voice
7. ___ Passive-aggressiveness
8. ___ Passive resistance (slowing down of movements)
9. ___ Difficulty getting to sleep or not sleeping through the night
10. ___ Repetitive disturbing or frightening dreams
11. ___ Grinding teeth, especially when sleeping

12. ___ Clenched jaw, including when sleeping

13. ___ Fist clenching, foot tapping, and facial tics

14. ___ Stomach problems

15. ___ Overeating, or undereating

16. ___ Frequent headaches

17. ___ Stiff or sore neck and shoulders, backache

18. ___ Chronic depression

19. ___ Feeling despair or discouragement

20. ___ Suicidal thoughts

21. ___ Lack of interest in life, including favorite pastimes

22. ___ Boredom

23. ___ Excessive impatience or irritability

24. ___ Obsessing about, or not letting go of unfair situations

25. ___ Regularly feeling victimized

26. ___ Frequently feeling inadequate

27. ___ Frequently feeling powerless

28. ___ Frequently feeling humiliated

29. ___ Frequently feeling ignored or not listened to

30. ___ Frequently feeling unappreciated

31. ___ Feeling detached or disconnected from other people

32. ___ Frequent breakups or divorces

33. ___ Frequent accidents

34. ___ Physically/verbally hurting someone unintentionally

35. ___ Frequently feeling guilty

36. ___ Road anger or road rage

37. ___ Checking out, not being present

38. ___ Frequent crying

39. ___ Frequent swearing

40. ___ Frequent altercations with others

41. ___ Frequent speeding or traffic tickets

42. ___ Frequent lawsuits

43. ___ Frequently feeling threatened

44. ___ Frequently fearful

45. ___ Not getting along with coworkers or bosses

46.___ Frequent job turnover
47.___ Self-loathing
48.___ Frequent negative thinking about life and others
49.___ Wanting to break or throw something
50.___ Excessive use of alcohol or other substances

This checklist may represent symptoms of other mental or medical conditions, but having ten or more checkmarks usually indicates hidden anger. Please consult a mental health counselor or physician if ever in doubt. Otherwise, own your anger, express it appropriately, and use it as a tool for more effective coping. And, by *appropriately*, I mean your expression of anger should be skillful, well-intentioned, well-modulated, useful, and timely.

8
Protect Yourself and Let Go of Your Anger

Off the Northwest coast of the United States is an archipelago called the San Juan Islands. From one of the mountaintops, you can see Canada, the United States mainland, and all the little islands in the San Juan chain. Lush vegetation and abundant wildlife characterize these glorious islands.

People come from all over the world to enjoy this magnificent view, so when attendance dropped dramatically, the park ranger went out to discover what was wrong. Standing at the park entrance was a proud buckskin mustang biting and kicking anyone who dared come near.

The park ranger approached the wild horse and, with great authority in his voice, said, "If you don't stop biting and kicking the visitors, I'll have you relocated to a zoo." An intelligent animal, the horse realized the ranger meant business and vowed not to display any aggressive behavior.

The tourists came back in droves, but when the ranger went to check on the horse, he found him beaten down and depressed. His once beautiful mane and tail had lost their luster, and he no longer carried himself with dignity. On questioning, the horse explained that children had pulled his tail and people had thrown rocks and mud balls at him.

"Why didn't you defend yourself?" the ranger asked.

Dejectedly, the mustang answered, "Because you told me you'd ship me to a zoo if I bit or kicked the tourists."

"Yes," the ranger acknowledged. "But that doesn't mean that you can't flick your tail, flatten your ears, stomp your foot, or snort through your nose. This will let them know they can't abuse you."

This story, which I call "The Zen of Horse Sense," teaches us to use anger to protect ourselves without harming others. Anger is constructive when used in this way, and self-expression can lead to relief. But, some people struggle to let go of anger and can't because they fear they will be vulnerable to being hurt again. When my clients voice this concern, I tell them, "If you have the right skills for protection, you can let go of your anger." Here are the skills:

1. **Get your facts straight.** Collect your information about people in reality, and take your time doing it. Ask yourself, "Is this person safe?" That way, you won't go off half-cocked.

2. **Speak up about your needs.** Let people know what your boundaries are and what you want or expect from them. Write out or practice how you want to deliver the information.

3. **Walk away from hurtful situations.** Disengage from escalating circumstances, and wait for things to cool down.

4. **God never hurt you.** That's not how God operates. You do not have to protect yourself from him. Yes, God allows bad things to happen to good people, but that does not make it his intention. If you believe God hurt you, reexamine your beliefs, grieve your situation, and move on.

5. **Have realistic expectations of what another person can and will do.** Don't set yourself up for hurt and anger by expecting an abusive person to be kind and considerate.

6. **Remember, we live in a gray world.** Black-and-white thinking is a dangerous game. Evaluate others as whole persons, and don't just write them off for one aspect of their personality.

7. **Set limits to ensure your safety.** You are a different person, stronger and wiser because you learn from your mistakes and operate in reality. If someone is standing on your toes, tell that person to get off!

8. **Use your "Adult" part rather than your inner "Child" to handle matters of vulnerability.** Your "Child" may be incapable of self-expression in situations where your "Adult" knows just what to say and how to say it. By contrast, your "Child" part may express itself in ways that actually make matters worse.

Protect Yourself Worksheet

Use this worksheet in any situation where you are angry and need to protect yourself. Where appropriate, write your thoughts and feelings under each of the eight protection skills.

1. **Get your facts straight.**

   _____

   _____

   _____

   _____

2. **Speak up about your needs.**

   _____

   _____

   _____

   _____

3. **Walk away from hurtful situations.**

   _____

   _____

   _____

   _____

4. **God never hurt you; let go.**

   _____

   _____

   _____

   _____

5. Have realistic expectations of other people.

_____

_____

_____

_____

6. Evaluate the person as a whole.

_____

_____

_____

_____

7. What are your limits?

_____

_____

_____

_____

8. How can you be mature about this? What would your strategy be to engage with the other person?

_____

_____

_____

_____

9
The Art of Waiting

"Siddhartha," he said, "why are you waiting?"
"You know why."
"Will you go on standing and waiting until it is day, noon, evening?"
"I will stand and wait."
"You will grow tired, Siddhartha."
"I will grow tired."
"You will fall asleep, Siddhartha."
"I will not fall asleep."
"You will die, Siddhartha."
"I will die."

—Hermann Hesse

Hermann Hesse, the German-born Swiss novelist, completed *Siddhartha* in 1922, but it took eleven years to write. If you have not read this deeply moving journey of self-discovery, I urge you to do so. In the passage above, young Siddhartha informs his father he is leaving his family and his religion, giving up an idyllic existence for the life of a wandering ascetic. He has performed all the religious rituals of his father's upper-caste Brahmin faith but has not attained happiness or inner peace. He even meets Buddha but decides his own enlightenment must come from his own experience. He becomes a ferryman and learns his teacher is the river itself ("the river knows everything"). On the path to enlightenment, Siddhartha discovers one of his most important lessons is to learn to wait skillfully.

What, exactly, does it mean to wait? Most often, it means to remain in a state of expectation. We wait for the elevator, wait for the flight to depart, wait for our paychecks, wait for the medicine to kick in, and some of us wait for "Mr. Right." As you might guess from these examples, waiting is seldom fun and often accompanied by a lower state of consciousness.

Don't believe me? Think of waiting for the traffic light to change when you're in a hurry, waiting for a stall in the ladies' room when you're desperate, or—worse yet—waiting "on hold" to speak with a real person after navigating an annoying phone tree for ten minutes. In each instance, it is quite easy to descend into our lower selves.

In the spiritual sense, waiting is a lesson. We must learn to wait in order to learn patience and equanimity. This was Siddhartha's insight, which views waiting as an opportunity, a space to breathe mindfully and notice what is happening in our bodies and minds. If we can learn to wait skillfully, waiting can be a blessing. If we become impatient, waiting will feel like a curse.

Consider a pregnant woman waiting for her baby to arrive. If she greets her experience with patience, the waiting becomes an acceptable part of life. If she resists what is happening and fights her discomfort, she will suffer more. If she embraces her experience with an open heart, she will be more at ease.

Herein lies Siddhartha's art of waiting. If we go with the flow and accept our circumstances, we are more peaceful. If we kick and scream and complain instead of waiting skillfully, we only make a difficult situation worse. It should be apparent that waiting skillfully is necessary to cope effectively with the stresses of modern life. Consider the following situations and think about how much less you will suffer if you learn the art of waiting:

- Learning to play the piano or another musical instrument.
- Losing the ten pounds you gained over the holidays.
- Grieving the loss of a loved family member, friend, or pet.
- Carrying and delivering your first baby.
- Healing from knee surgery so you can resume working out.

Get it? All of these experiences will be infinitely more stressful if you can't wait. So, how do we learn to wait more skillfully? We practice, and we ask ourselves the following questions:

- "Is this wait worth getting angry about?"
- "Is my impatience worth harming my physical and mental health?"
- "Is this wait going to last forever?"
- "Can I let go or focus on something else while I wait?"
- "Can I consciously slow myself down in the interest of inner peace?"
- "Is the situation I find myself in really so urgent?"

Once we've answered these questions, we can adopt some other strategies to master the art of waiting.

1. Bring and read a book or magazine.
2. Look at your calendar or appointment book.
3. Make plans for forthcoming events.
4. Write a list for chores, shopping, Christmas, or phone calls.
5. Listen to music or a book on tape.
6. Think about something pleasant from the past, present, or future.
7. Remember to breathe properly (slowly and deeply).
8. Knit or crochet.
9. Play a game.
10. Pray.
11. Have a healthy snack.
12. Have a cup of tea.
13. Make a gift list for your friend or partner.
14. Enjoy the pleasure of people-watching.
15. Buy a nice set of prayer beads, and learn to use them.

The art of waiting is really about accepting the reality that life doesn't always go our way. Acceptance here does not mean we approve of or resign ourselves to what is or isn't happening; it doesn't mean we enjoy waiting or give in to adversity. It means we stop fighting what is and make peace with the present. Waiting skillfully is surrendering, embracing the present moment just as it is.

Imagine you're standing in line at the grocery store, and the person in front of you is writing a check at a pace slower than cold molasses moves. It's been a long day, and you want to get home. If you fight it, roll your eyes, and think to yourself how inconsiderate and stupid people are, you will be miserable. If you take a deep breath and practice patience, you will maintain your inner peace. From this position, you can act with equanimity. You could calmly ask if another checkout line could be opened or just breathe and let go of your attachment to making the experience go faster.

Imagine how much easier your life will be once you learn the art of waiting. Read *Siddhartha*! Now practice your new waiting skills. I guarantee you will be given plenty of opportunities.

All things come to him who waits—provided he knows what he is waiting for.
—Woodrow Wilson

10
Managing Depression
(A Step in the Right Direction)

The term clinical depression finds its way into too many conversations these days. One has a sense that a catastrophe has occurred in the psychic landscape.

—Leonard Cohen

Mysteriously and in ways that are totally remote from natural experience, the gray drizzle of horror induced by depression takes on the quality of physical pain.

—William Styron

Preventing and managing depression requires effort and aim in terms of self-care. Naturally, you need to know if you are, in fact, depressed, because many people are unaware the illness is happening to them. They get used to it and assume it's just the way folks feel, part of life. Here are some signals that will help you make an accurate assessment of your mood. When you suffer from depression, you:

1. Spend a lot of time crying and feeling blue.
2. Tend to feel helpless and hopeless.
3. Either lose your appetite and lose weight or overeat to comfort yourself and gain weight.
4. Either can't sleep or oversleep to avoid your feelings.
5. Lose your energy and motivation.
6. Lose your sex drive.

7. Lose interest in the activities and hobbies that usually give you pleasure.
8. Isolate yourself from friends and family.
9. Feel irritable and angry and have a short fuse.
10. Notice your self-esteem plummeting, e.g., you feel unworthy, unlovable, undeserving, self-critical, and defective.
11. Find it hard to concentrate and may have memory lapses.
12. May develop unexplained aches and pains.
13. Might engage in reckless behavior that is uncharacteristic for you, e.g., substance abuse, impulsive spending, reckless driving.
14. May have thoughts that life is no longer worth living and think of suicide (if this one fits, you *must* seek professional help immediately).

Women are twice as likely to become depressed as men. While this is partly due to hormones, I believe the primary factors are because our culture doesn't give women equal rights and power and also because of higher rates of childhood trauma, particularly sexual abuse. Men are certainly not immune from depression but hide it from themselves and others because they see it as a sign of weakness. Whereas depressed women tend to overeat, oversleep, and lose their sexual drive, depressed men show irritability, fatigue, and loss of interest in activities they typically find pleasurable, e.g., hanging out with buddies, tinkering around the house, exercising, or watching sports on TV.

In general, whether you're male or female, the causes or triggers of depression are:

- A family history of neglect, substance abuse, or abandonment
- A family history of depression or another mood disorder
- A history of childhood physical or sexual abuse
- Trauma, such as assault or rape
- Serious couple or relationship problems
- Feeling lonely or empty

- Addiction to drugs or alcohol
- Unemployment
- Financial stress
- Onset of illness or chronic pain
- A blow to self-esteem, e.g., left in a relationship, fired from work
- Death of a friend or family member, loss of pets

Gina, a physician in her forties, had several of the risk factors cited here. Her mother had suffered from depression, and Gina was molested as a child by her junior high school track coach. In addition, she was conflicted in her marriage and sought refuge by drinking too much wine. Ironically, she knew a lot about depression from a medical standpoint but prior to treatment with me, had decided on medications alone.

Our treatment plan focused on making lifestyle changes, which led to Gina exercising regularly, eating more nutritional food, cutting down to one glass of wine per evening, taking vitamin supplements, meditating twenty minutes a day for stress reduction, and building a better support system.

We also taught her to deal with her negative thoughts about herself and to greet them differently when they came up. For instance, she disputed thoughts like "I'm a terrible wife," by recognizing the reality that she wasn't or she detached from them by just watching the thoughts and realizing that just because her mind produced the thoughts didn't make them true.

Moreover, I encouraged Gina to get into the habit of doing wonderful things for herself and to convince herself she deserved it. She would make a list for daily practice, put the activities on a calendar, and make them as important as going to the hospital where she worked. Now she regularly got massages, attended a book club, walked her dog, and enjoyed dinner dates or movies with her female friends. In six months of committing to the process, she was sufficiently free from her depression that she could discontinue the antidepressant medications.

Managing Depression Checklist

(Warning Signs)

___ Withdrawing
___ Avoiding people
___ Feeling lonely
___ Feeling critical
___ Feeling criticized
___ Feeling like no one understands
___ Lack of interest in usually fun activities
___ Being unable to accomplish normal activities
___ An inability to show affection
___ Low libido (sex drive)
___ Inability to experience pleasure
___ Talking less
___ Being void of emotion
___ Low self-esteem
___ Being unproductive
___ Feeling insecure
___ Being inactive
___ Feeling despondent
___ Being low energy
___ Having trouble getting dressed
___ Feeling dependent
___ Slowed speech
___ Crying easily
___ Experiencing extreme sadness
___ Having inappropriate guilt
___ Engaging in risky behavior
___ Having self-destructive thoughts

___ Experiencing suicidal ideation (thinking, talking, planning, or attempting)
___ Feeling like giving up on life
___ Having a negative attitude
___ Feeling irritable, angry
___ Becoming easily frustrated
___ Experiencing agitation
___ Having anxiety, worry, or irrational fears
___ Feeling bored
___ Sleeping excessively
___ Waking early
___ Suffering insomnia
___ Remaining in bed for long periods of time
___ Having problems concentrating
___ Having a poor memory
___ Feeling confused
___ Feeling disorganized
___ Feeling overwhelmed by finances
___ Feeling overwhelmed by personal problems
___ Reasoning ability slowing
___ Exhibiting paranoia
___ Overeating
___ Undereating
___ Feeling nauseous
___ Eating junk food
___ Craving carbohydrates (especially sugar)
___ Increasing consumption of alcohol
___ Using illicit drugs
___ Overusing prescription medications
___ Having headaches
___ Having back and neck aches
___ Experiencing aching joints
___ Trembling
___ Senses shutting down

___ Feeling numb
___ Can't bring yourself to do physical exercise
___ Being clumsy, accident prone

Depression Management and Prevention

(Fifty Large Things to Do)

1. Plan a trip or vacation.
2. Go on a trip or vacation.
3. Go to a church.
4. Go to a library.
5. Go to a movie.
6. Go to a play.
7. Go to a comedy.
8. Read a poem, or write your own.
9. Exercise inside or outside.
10. Take your dog for a walk.
11. Play with your animals.
12. Go for a horseback ride.
13. Pop some popcorn.
14. Journal your feelings.
15. Set a modest goal, and achieve it.
16. Take a car or a bike ride.
17. Take a day hike.
18. Do some yardwork or gardening.
19. Join a club or a group.
20. Take a class (brick and mortar or online).
21. Take a walk or jog.
22. Start a new hobby.
23. Fly a kite.
24. Visit with friends or family.
25. Have people over.
26. Watch your children or someone you know participate in sports.

27. Tell someone you love him or her.
28. Find some reason to laugh.
29. Buy tickets and see your favorite sports team.
30. Buy tickets and see your favorite musical group.
31. See local sights, such as the zoo, waterfront, mountains, beach, or a gallery.
32. Go places to look for fun, such as shops, parks, home tours, fairs, and parades.
33. Go to a car or horse race.
34. Volunteer at a place you would enjoy.
35. Swim, camp, or fish.
36. Get a massage.
37. Clean up a room.
38. Clean up your car.
39. Read a book on spiritual development.
40. Take a bus tour.
41. Take a boat or ferry ride.
42. Cook a new meal for yourself.
43. Refinish a piece of furniture.
44. Draw or design something.
45. Build something.
46. Fix or tinker with something around the house.
47. Paint a room a fun color.
48. Chop some wood.
49. Go dancing.
50. Try something new; be open to it.

Managing Depression

(Fifty Small Things to Do)

1. Have a cup of tea, herbal or regular, depending on the time of day.
2. Make use of your reclining chair or rocker.
3. Take a hot bubble bath, herbal bath, or shower.
4. Sit with your animals.
5. Wrap yourself in your favorite blanket.
6. Read a good book, newspaper, or magazine.
7. Watch a favorite movie.
8. Listen to a quiet moment.
9. Work on your favorite hobby; if you don't have one, start one.
10. Listen to the rain on the roof.
11. Call or e-mail a favorite friend or relative.
12. Write a letter to a friend.
13. Write down what you are grateful for.
14. List fun plans for the day/week, and put them on a calendar.
15. Do a jigsaw or crossword puzzle.
16. Sew, knit, or do needlepoint.
17. Garden in the yard, in pots, or on the deck.
18. Repair things in the home that are simple.
19. Bake something with a sugar substitute.
20. Cook soup or something nutritious.
21. Drink juice or eat fruit.
22. Get flowers, and put them around the house—or plant them.
23. Burn candles, sage, or incense.
24. Listen to uplifting music.
25. Go for a drive.
26. Sit in front of a warm fire.
27. Play your favorite board game.
28. Watch the birds or animals outside your window.

29. Play an instrument.
30. Rearrange the furniture.
31. Cry.
32. Laugh.
33. Do something pleasurable on the computer.
34. Do something creative.
35. Take a hot shower.
36. Paint your toenails.
37. Dance.
38. Sing.
39. Rearrange your drawers.
40. Do something nice for someone.
41. Enjoy the fresh air.
42. Get a back rub.
43. Look at a window display.
44. Watch the sun set.
45. Remember fun experiences.
46. Stretch your body.
47. Look at photographs, frame them, or put them in albums.
48. Make a friend laugh.
49. Buy an inexpensive toy, and play with it.
50. Create a simple diversion, and carry it out.

11
One Is the Loneliest Number— Celebrating Alone Time

One is the loneliest number that you will ever do
Two can be as bad as one
It's the loneliest number since the number one

—Three Dog Night

For some, alone time is an extravagant luxury, an opportunity to rejuvenate the body, mind and spirit. But for others, being alone can be a time of feeling painfully empty and cut off from meaningful relationships without hope of reconnection. What differentiates the one experience from the other is whether we can be good company to ourselves and be happy regardless of whether we are by ourselves or sharing time with another. Each person has their own uniquely optimal balance of separateness and togetherness, and the trick is to respond creatively to either too little or too much time alone.

Let's examine each situation and consider solutions to whichever problem you face, keeping in mind that they may change over time or even during the course of a day.

Too Little Time Alone

1. Select ten to thirty minutes during the day when you can be by yourself. Some people find it easier to plan for the same time period every day, and others find it easier to plan each day individually.

Decide what works best for you, and take time to meditate, pray, walk in nature, relax in the tub, or listen to music that moves you.

2. Anticipate problems or interruptions that might interfere with your alone time. Educate those around you (family, friends, and people at work) that you have scheduled this time, and request uninterrupted privacy. Should they fail to honor your request, stand firm and be consistent in guarding your time and space.

3. Create a resource list of things you could do to renew yourself. Remember, the idea is to give yourself a meaningful gift. Put as many things on the list as you can think of and keep adding to the list. Not allowed are unnecessary sleep, television or radio (unless it is uplifting or inspiring music), chores, letters, telephone calls, or activities involving other people.

Too Much Time Alone

1. Make a list of family and friends with whom you'd like to spend more time. Contact those on your list, make clear your wish to see them, and plan a get-together. Yes, you will feel vulnerable asking for what you want. Yes, they might disappoint you or reject your offer. Life isn't about playing it safe all the time. Getting what you need is often about taking good risks.

2. Decide how you would most like to connect with new friends. Would it be meeting for coffee, going for a walk, or taking in that new *movie* everyone is talking about? What will work best for you to give you the feeling that you belong? Would it be joining a church, a book club, a Yoga class, a support group, the PTA, or volunteering for a nonprofit organization?

3. Plan ahead to deal with problems or feelings that might get in the way of carrying out the activities that would make you feel better.

Have a plan B. Don't give in to procrastination, negative moods, lack of interest, or low energy. Once you plan it, *do it*! Stand up to the part of you that feels lazy, anxious, or stuck.

Make it a point to regularly check in with yourself to see if you want or need more separateness, or more togetherness. There's no one right way or one healthy way to do alone time or together time, there's what's right or healthy for you as you seek the balance that makes you happy and fulfilled. This will be based on your unique temperament, personality type, attachment history, trauma history, relationship status, current social circumstances and many other factors. So checking in means paying attention to your thoughts, feelings and needs around either connecting with or withdrawing from others. Yes, withdrawal from others is healthy when it supports what you want or need and you do not have to apologize for needing to withdraw.

If you're feeling lonely or isolated, or if you're feeling boredom, or if something wonderful has happened and you want to share the experience, or if something really awful has happened and you need some emotional support, reach out to a friend, family member or some appropriate person. Strive to be with them in an authentic way so that you truly connect, as opposed to not really being both present and transparent and then leaving dissatisfied. This, of course, requires that you feel safe with the person you've chosen to connect with.

On the other hand, if you feel intruded upon or smothered by someone, or if you feel bothered by the drama or toxicity of those around you, or if you've simply been around people too much of late, give yourself the benefit of some much needed space. Try to savor the experience of peaceful aloneness by letting go of whatever stress you've taken on and really appreciating life. You do this by noticing the weird energy that's accumulated in your body and then relaxing your heart, loosening all the tight spots in your body, taking some deep down into the tummy breaths and releasing that unwanted energy as you exhale. Then, do it again and again until you begin to regain a sense of feeling calm and centered.

Herein lies the secret to celebrating alone time... you release the negative energy that's contaminated your body, mind and spirit, and restore yourself to a state of inner peace where you simply enjoy life. Now you are free. This means you can either be alone or you can be with others because you know how to balance both experiences in a way that makes you happy.

A wise man is never less alone than when alone.

—Proverb

12
Sleep Hygiene

That we are not much sicker and much madder than we are is due exclusively to that most blessed and blessing of all natural graces, sleep.

—Aldous Huxley

Sleep that knits up the raveled sleeve of care
The death of each day's life, sore labour's bath
Balm of hurt minds, great nature's second course,
Chief nourisher in life's feast.

—William Shakespeare

Sleep is the golden chain that ties health and our bodies together.

—Thomas Dekker

"Go to bed. Get your sleep!" your parents lectured, but most of us, at least in the teenage years, preferred to stay up till all hours of the night. OK, so you're not a restless teen anymore, but do you get enough sleep?

The National Sleep Foundation recommends we get eight hours a night. Many of us get less given the demands of work and family, the lure of exciting social activities, page-turner novels, the daily stresses of a frantic modern society, the noise from always-on television, non-stop access to the Internet, and, of course, Facebook and other social media.

So you're not "tired" or "sleepy," why not just shave off an hour of sleep? If you can't relax physically when you get between the sheets, you shave off another hour. You've had too much caffeine or are unable to "turn off" your mind, so you go to bed an hour late. Your thoughts morph into worry, guilt, anger, or self-condemnation, and you lose another hour on that night, too. See what's happening? Pretty soon, you've accumulated a hefty "sleep debt," which is the cumulative effect of being sleep deprived, resulting in mental and physical fatigue.

"The brain keeps an exact accounting of how much sleep it is owed," according to Dr. William C. Dement, the pioneering sleep researcher at Stanford University. This means we pay dearly for sleep debt, especially in terms of productivity. Not only do people do less, but they start making mistakes, sometimes with enormous consequences. Sleep deprivation was cited as a "direct cause" in the 1986 space shuttle *Challenger* explosion, which killed seven astronauts, as well as the 1989 *Exxon Valdez* thirty-million-gallon oil spill in the ocean off Alaska. Obviously, your sleep-deprived mistakes probably won't have consequences like that, but they could cause you to miss time at work, have a car accident, botch an important task, or overreact and say something insensitive to someone close.

A sleeping mind is a busy mind, and this is why proper sleep is crucial to effective coping. During sleep, the brain records memories, processes newly learned information, sorts out and discards unneeded information, works out life stress through vivid dream imagery, and sends out complex signals and sophisticated hormones that repair and replace the body's cells. Obviously, we need to learn to turn the day off and prepare ourselves for sleep. Start by assessing your own sleep needs and developing a plan to ensure you meet your requirements:

1. **Figure out your own personal sleep budget.** People typically need an hour of sleep for every two hours awake, which computes to the recommended eight hours a night. But everyone's different. Teens certainly need more sleep than that, and as you age, you might need less. Optimal sleep time will allow you to awake refreshed and rejuvenated; too much sleep will leave you feeling groggy. During times of added stress, depression, or unusually heavy physical activity, you should add an additional thirty to forty-five minutes.

2. **Create a one-hour "buffer zone" between the end of the day's activities and retiring to bed.** This will provide a quiet period to wind down and prepare the body and mind for restful sleep. Do select peaceful, quiet, and enjoyable activities to fill this time. Pamper yourself with a bath or soothing music, and feel gratitude for the day's blessings. Don't watch TV, do crossword puzzles, or read in bed. Bed is for sleep or lovemaking.

3. **Go to bed on time, and develop a sleep ritual by going to bed at the same time every night!** Figure your bedtime by counting back from the time you have to get up in the morning and adding in another twenty minutes for dropping off to sleep. If you need to get up at 7:00 a.m. and your sleep budget calls for eight hours of sleep, go to bed at 10:40 p.m.

4. **If you have trouble falling asleep, don't fret.** As Dale Carnegie reminds us, it's the worry that gets us, not the lack of sleep. Instead of worrying, try effortless diaphragmatic breathing. Just close your eyes and pay attention to your breaths; notice how your tummy rises as you breathe in and falls as you breathe out. Allow your body to breathe itself, and then let it gradually slow your breathing down. Be certain you are breathing deep down. Or do a breathing meditation by focusing on your breathing pattern and counting each breath. When you get to ten, start over. If it works better for you to engage in pleasant daydreaming or prayer, try that.

Here are a few more tips for turning sleep into a blessing:

- Get more exercise, especially in the late afternoon or evening, but not right before bedtime.

- Discover your optimal sleeping conditions, e.g., room temperature, some fresh air, white noise or no noise, door locked, quality mattress and pillow, and so on.

- If you awaken early, make any corrections to increase your comfort and chance of falling back asleep. If, after fifteen minutes, you cannot fall asleep, get up and do an unpleasant chore, e.g., clean the bathroom, polish the silver, fold the laundry, and so on, and then return to bed.

- If you are sleeping too much, you are probably feeling overwhelmed, so figure out what things could be postponed, delegated, or dropped altogether.

- Write out a "to-do" list so you can let go at bedtime and not worry about forgetting things that you have to do.

- Eliminate caffeine, alcohol, and nicotine, especially in the evening hours.

- Sniff a soothing scent before retiring. Jasmine or lavender-scented rooms have promoted sleep for thousands of years.

- Slow, soft classical music before bedtime can slow your heartbeat and breathing, thus enhancing sleep. New Age music without any lyrics also works.

- A shower or a bath will wash away the day's stressors and prepare you for restful sleep.

- Prayer or meditation before bedtime will enhance sleep, but remember the words of the Dalai Lama, "Sleep is the best meditation."

- If your partner's snoring interferes, either take care of the snoring issue or sleep in a different room. Find other times to cuddle or make love.

In conclusion, I offer a few words about the twenty-minute "power nap," sometimes called a catnap or midday sleep. This is a wonderful opportunity whenever you've accumulated a sleep deficit, burned out from too rigorous a schedule, worked long hours, traveled between time zones, or just need an extra lift. Try not to go past twenty minutes, as this might put you into deep sleep and then sleep inertia, or leave you feeling groggy. If this happens, splash cold water on your face, exercise briefly, or allow yourself a jolt of caffeine. In the words of Edward Lucas, "There is more refreshment and stimulation in a nap, even of the briefest, than in all the alcohol ever distilled."

Ensuring a good night's sleep is a basic life skill that makes good coping possible. The benefits of proper sleep are less stress, more energy, enhanced mood, greater productivity, increased learning, improved memory, and better health. When we become sleep deprived, we reverse these benefits and our emotional challenges become magnified—small stresses become big, and bigger stresses become overwhelming. When we've had a good night's sleep, we see the world through different eyes.

13
Recharging
(You and the Energizer Bunny)

Energy and persistence conquer all things.

—Benjamin Franklin

Love the moment and the energy of that moment will spread beyond all boundaries.

—Sister Mary Corita Kent

The Eveready Energizer Bunny first hopped onto TV in 1989 and soon became an advertising icon. With hot-pink fur and dark shades, this cool rabbit kept on "going and going and going." After outlasting a number of popular toys, he took on King Kong, Darth Vader, and Wile E. Coyote and bested them, too. Don't you wish you had some of the Energizer Bunny's energy? Keep reading. You can.

Recharging your battery is really a mind-body management skill—and an important one at that. Even the Energizer Bunny eventually runs out of energy, and so do we. At such times, we need to recharge ourselves, and the best way to do this is to know what's worked in the past. Some women end up chronically exhausted or burned out and don't know why. Typically, they are disconnected from themselves, don't notice the warning signs of early fatigue or boredom, and end up depleted. It's like turning off a switch.

Marie was like this, lacking energy but not connected with herself and not knowing why. A baker, she was extremely busy on the job and, by necessity, had to start her day in the wee hours of the morning. The problem was she also worked late and had trouble setting limits with a demanding supervisor at the bakery. To make matters worse, she never did anything for herself even when she did have time. When I asked what she did to recharge herself, she replied, "What do you mean?" She literally had no idea of what I was talking about but fortunately was open to learning to take better care of herself.

Below is Marie's list of activities that would recharge her if she took the time to do them. She agreed to set aside not less than thirty minutes a day for one of the activities on her list. After doing this for a month, she reported her depression had lifted, she slept better, she got more pleasure out of life, she reported greater job satisfaction, and she had more energy.

Marie's list:

1. Visit an art gallery.
2. Browse a cooking magazine.
3. Meditate for fifteen to thirty minutes.
4. Go antiquing with friends.
5. Travel or go on vacation.
6. Take a brisk walk.
7. Ride a horse.
8. Play with an animal.
9. Do Yoga or Qi Gong (energy exercises).
10. Work out at home or the gym.
11. Listen to my favorite music.
12. Make love with my partner.
13. Take a power nap.
14. Take a cool shower.
15. Make iced tea with lemon.
16. Call a friend and laugh.
17. Go on a day trip.
18. Find a beach and walk it.
19. Imagine walking along a beach.
20. Dance with no one watching.

Your list may look completely different. I only include this as an example of the types of activities that can be energizing. List your favorite recharging activities that have worked for you or that might work for you. Be creative and willing to try something new, even if you're unsure how it would suit you. Be willing to experiment. If you try out hot Yoga or training for a running event and don't like your experience, try something else. Keep trying until you find your own Energizer Bunny within. Have your list handy when you need reminders to refresh yourself. Your list can be used in conjunction with "Managing Depression" and "Sleep Hygiene" (see these chapters, 10 and 12, respectively, for suggestions).

Recharging Worksheet

Your personal ideas for reenergizing yourself:

1. _____

2. _____

3. _____

4. _____

5. _____

6. _____

7. _____

8. _____

9. _____

10. _____

11. _____

12. _____

14
Working through Grief and Loss

He who has felt the deepest grief is best able to experience supreme happiness.
—Alexandre Dumas

Grief is like the ocean; it comes on waves ebbing and flowing. Sometimes the water is calm, and sometimes it is overwhelming. All we can do is learn to swim.

—Vicki Harrison

All of us must face grief at some time in our life. A loss of some sort will occur—perhaps a separation from someone we loved, having to relocate and part from dear friends, or the death of a beloved pet—and we will suffer mental anguish and deep sorrow. There are many ways of coping with grief, some healthy, some unhealthy, but there are some common stages most people experience.

Elisabeth Kübler-Ross, a Swiss psychiatrist who studied the process of grief and near-death experiences, outlined five stages:

1. **Denial** — "I'm *OK*, really." "Is this really happening?" "I can't believe this is happening to me."
2. **Anger** — "This is not fair!" "Why me?" "What did I do?" "I don't deserve this."
3. **Bargaining** — "Whatever I have to do I'll do it if it means I don't die." "I'll never say another mean word to anyone if I get what I'm asking for."
4. **Depression** — "What's the use in going on?" "There's nothing to live for any more." "Without my loved one, I can't go on."

5. **Acceptance** — "I can accept what is." "I can do this, with help and support from others." "I surrender to the reality of what has happened." "It is what it is." "I don't have to like it but I can accept it."

Grief gets complicated, and not all people believe the stages apply to their experience of loss. The stages are not always in sequence, and there are variations where you might experience two stages but skip three. Some people also feel numb, guilty, or even relieved, depending on circumstances. Women more often go through all the stages compared to men.

This chapter addresses the issues that are most commonly seen when people become stuck and fail to reach the all-important acceptance stage. Acceptance means coming to terms with the loss, being able to move on and reinvest your life energy.

Grieving has a rhythm similar to the waves in an ocean. There are big waves that come when we are reminded of the loss we are grieving, sometimes even a tsunami if it is the anniversary of a loved one's death. There are smaller waves that come as well, most often with memories that pop up for whatever reason. If we can come to understand how we process our grief, it becomes much less painful. We don't need to be afraid of the experience or feel out of control; it is simply a natural process. Just as the body knows how to heal a wound to the skin, the mind and spirit know how to heal a wound to the psyche through mourning.

One of the biggest things people grieve is the loss of their hopes and dreams. Many times, people don't realize how important these losses are and discount the power and energy of their experience. It seems easier to grieve the loss of a person or an animal than it does to grieve the loss of a hope, dream, or youthful innocence. Unless you take time to be with yourself, feel the layers of feelings, and let them pass through you, you can slip into depression.

Whereas depression may seem to come from a bottomless well, grief is more like a reservoir we can drain by crying out the tears and getting comfort from others. This means we must make time to grieve, because if we push it down, the energy will remain in our bodies and find expression in ways that are not productive. Suppressed grief tends to come out in uncontrollable crying, physical symptoms, inappropriate anger, accidents, loss of energy, forgetfulness, lack of focus, and disconnection from our loved ones or ourselves.

Meredith came to therapy shortly after losing her father to lung cancer in his late sixties. She seemed stuck in the Depression phase of grieving and could not get to Acceptance. On exploring her feelings about why she was stuck, she told me she had argued her entire life with her father about his cigarette smoking. Now she felt furious at him for not quitting the habit and taking better care of himself, but at the same time, she felt guilty because she believed it was not OK to be mad at someone who'd just passed away. In effect, her guilt blocked the release of her anger and kept her from moving on. After several sessions, she realized it was normal and natural for her to be mad at her deceased father and she could then vent her feelings. Behind the anger was a profound heartache that eased with the release of her tears. Here are some of the tools we used to help Meredith resolve her grief:

1. **Comfort yourself through your "learned history of grief."** "I've been through grief before, and I can survive it again. I don't have to like it, but I know it will not last forever."

2. **Get to know your "personal rhythm of grief."** "Wow. I just got hit with another wave of grief and have to ride it out. It won't last forever. I'm going to let the feelings pass through me."

3. **Become aware of anniversary dates, activities, and circumstances that generate waves of grief.** Prepare yourself by setting aside extra personal time and planning for extra comfort and support when you know you are especially vulnerable.

4. **Practice supportive self-talk during times of intense grieving.** "Why am I feeling this way? Oh, that's right; I'm grieving." "These feelings won't last forever. I've grieved before and survived it; I can do it again." "I don't have to be alone when going through this painful experience. Whom can I contact?" "What do I need or want to feel some relief? What can I do to take better care of myself?"

5. **Take care of yourself when the waves of grief hit.** Cut back on your schedule, and be gentle with yourself. Write in a journal, talk to friends, or talk to a counselor. Read about the issue you are grieving, drink a cup of tea, rock in a rocking chair, cuddle with your pet, meditate, talk a walk in the garden, burn a candle, or complete a ritual (donate money to a good cause, plant a tree, or frame a special picture in memory of the loss). Surf the waves!

6. **Remember that new losses open old grief files.** If your dog dies, you not only grieve that loss but might also get into your loss files, unconsciously, and regrieve every pet you've lost in your life. Moreover, guilt, anger, fear, and sadness can cause you to become stuck. Many people are afraid to feel their feelings and try to cope by disconnecting from themselves. This could be nothing more than spacing out, but it could also include self-medication with alcohol, drugs, or other addictive behaviors. For those who had little or no support to grieve when they were younger or for those who are fearful they will be flooded with feelings and unable to function, grief presents a frightening experience. If this sounds like you, feel your feelings and let them pass through you. You can pace and modulate your emotions by using journals, unmailable letters, imagery (an example would be to imagine a faucet where you have control over the flow of water), rituals, talking in groups, or supporting others.

If you are fearful of feeling anger or get stuck in anger and don't know what to do with it, seek professional help. Counselors can provide support that will allow you to express your feelings more skillfully. (Please see the chapters on anger in this book).

Reframe the loss. Ask yourself:

- "What are the gifts, what have I learned that I can take with me?"
- "How can I grow from this painful experience and use it to my advantage?"
- "What am I supposed to learn? What is life teaching me?"

Examples of lessons you can learn include:

- Live each day to the fullest.
- In the words of singer/songwriter Warren Zevon on his deathbed, "Enjoy every sandwich!"
- Appreciate your loved ones and tell them you love them often.

Ask yourself the following questions:

- What mistakes have I made as I tried to work through this particular loss, and how can I do it differently next time?
- What special qualities or personal philosophy did this person have that I take with me?
- What can I do to honor the memory of this loss? Examples include write a book, take a trip, throw a party, donate a bench to a park, plant a tree or shrub as a memorial, donate money, or volunteer at a nonprofit organization.
- How can I develop and use a spiritual/philosophical belief system? Go to church, pray, and talk to your minister, rabbi, priest, or religious leader. Use the comfort of the congregation. Ask your Higher Power for support and guidance. Meditate, take a spiritual journey, smudge, or chant. These are only a few suggestions; there are many more (see chapter 41, "Something to Fall Back On").

The next time you find yourself grieving a loss, get out this list and work with each of the six tools; you will find comfort. Indeed, grief work can be painful, but it is an opportunity to learn acceptance, compassion, and wisdom.

15
Grieving the Lost Years

All efforts to heal the heart with the head fail because the head is the wrong tool for the job. It's like trying to paint with a hammer—it only makes a mess.
—John W. James and Russell Friedman

Waste not fresh tears over old griefs.

—Euripides

Grief is the feeling of deep sadness caused by the experience of a major loss. Our capacity for grieving is hardwired in the factory; it is a natural, normal, and healthy process aimed at restoring us to a state of equilibrium. There are many losses in childhood—leaving home to begin school, the death of a beloved pet, best friends moving out of state, parents separating or divorcing, leaving school and community upon graduation. Any or all of these experiences can leave us with a broken heart.

Having worked in counseling with many grievers, I have identified a particular loss I consider one of the most devastating, namely, not getting your emotional needs met by your parents or the person or persons who raised you. I refer to the time spent grieving such experiences as the "lost years." To complicate matters, unmet needs during the lost years lead to further losses, such as not having the coping skills to successfully manage your life or not having the educational opportunities to pursue your life purpose.

Those who have not recovered from their lost years often resort to emotional avoidance so as not to feel the unresolved grief. When triggered by life circumstances or old memories, they head for the liquor store for relief, escape via a drug of choice, or run to the refrigerator for comfort food. While these strategies might provide some short-term relief, they create a false illusion of coping and actually reinforce the problem in the long run.

Recovery means achieving a state of health by learning the coping skills you should have picked up as a child. It is not an easy process, but when you complete it, you will feel better because you've mended your broken heart. This means accepting the loss, completing the past, and moving on.

Conflicting feelings make grief work difficult. Suppose you move out of state to begin college and to feel free from a domineering parent who used guilt and intimidation to keep you close to home. This is all good, yes? No, not if you now feel overwhelming fear at your new freedom and independence because you never learned how to be on your own. To recover, you must learn the new skill of making independent choices and sound judgments about what to do, where to go, how to spend your money, and whom to call your friends.

Sometimes, we emerge from grieving lost years and discover unexpected gifts that emanate from the difficult experiences we endured. Let me explain through a personal example. As a child, my father heaped verbal abuse upon me. This often took place on the family farm in the presence of the hired hands. I was made to feel small and stupid and could have never imagined anything good could come from such humiliation. Now I realize there were gifts to be found in the suffering he inflicted. First, as a result of his harmful behavior, I made a sacred vow to choose my words carefully and avoid hurting those around me. Like the Buddhist concept of "right speech," I decided to communicate to others with compassion and respect.

While it is true I endured a great deal of criticism, I learned to work with my hands, to repair things, and to function as a general contractor in the building of homes. I learned how to relate to workmen and, by breaking my father's legacy, to speak to them in ways that bring out their best efforts. I'm not afraid to get my hands dirty or work late until the job is done. I discovered I love working on my own farm.

On an emotional level, I learned I did not have to carry my father's issues in the form of shame. He passed his shame to me, but I passed it back by working it through in my own therapy. Simply stated, his abusiveness was a commentary on him, not me. Sadly, he passed away without ever coming to terms with his own abusive childhood. I forgive him for the mean way he spoke to my siblings, my mother, and me. Even though his behavior was unacceptable by any standards, even though he harmed the ones he was supposed to love and support, I forgive him completely. His resources were limited, and he could only act upon what he was aware of at the time.

Grieving the Lost Years Worksheet

1. Parents' issues (alcoholism, divorce, neglect, immaturity, domestic violence, abuse, and so on):

_____

_____

_____

_____

2. Lack of opportunities (unstable home, many moves, poverty, poor guidance, and so on):

_____

_____

_____

_____

3. Mistakes made (acting-out behavior[1]):

_____

_____

_____

_____

4. Lack of awareness or coping skills:

_____

_____

_____

_____

---

1 Acting-out behavior is typically done under the influence of drugs or alcohol or any other untreated addiction or unresolved emotional issues, for example, losing the family home due to a gambling addiction, sexual promiscuity due to sexual abuse, cutting off family members because of childhood trauma that doesn't warrant cutting off, or self-harming behavior, like self-mutilation, instead of appropriate expression of emotion.

5. Forgiving self (see "About Forgiveness," chapter 18):

_____

_____

_____

_____

6. Make amends to significant others (see "Making Mistakes Skillfully" chapter 34):

_____

_____

_____

_____

7. Forgiving others:

_____

_____

_____

_____

8. Letting go:

_____

_____

_____

_____

9. Gifts or lessons:

_____

_____

_____

_____

It is not necessary to forgive to complete the healing process, only to let go.
—Stanley Wilson

There is more in us than we know. If we can be made to see it, perhaps, for the rest of our lives, we will be unwilling to settle for less.
—Kurt Hahn

16
Looking for the Gifts
and Opportunities

Difficulties mastered are opportunities won.

—Winston Churchill

I saw grief drinking a cup of sorrow and called out, "It tastes sweet, does it not?" "You've caught me," grief answered, "and you've ruined my business, how can I sell sorrow when you know it's a blessing?"

—Rumi

In the past few years, I have suffered numerous losses. As I went through the grief process in these dark moments, I began to look for gifts and opportunities. And I found them. When someone close to me has died, I think to myself, "What did I learn from this person?" "What impact did he or she have on my life or the lives of others?" From my father's passing, I learned that forgiveness relieves me of the terrible burden of resentment. My mother's death reminded me of my heartfelt appreciation for the home she made and to treasure her undying love. No matter how much pain there is in loss, there is always a lesson.

I have learned from people who have spent time with me before they passed. Those people have given me much to think about and have stimulated me to reevaluate my belief system. A woman mentor recently died. She was a medical doctor who returned to school in her seventies and did graduate work (so much for the adage about not being able to "teach old dogs new tricks"). Despite my friend's obvious brilliance and many accomplishments, she treated everyone she met with the utmost dignity and respect. She taught me to look for and find the inherent goodness in every human being, regardless of how they looked or acted. My mentor's stance toward others reminds me of a story about Mother Theresa, who referred to a filthy, vomit-covered homeless drunk as "Jesus in one of his many distressing disguises." When we can look past the flaws in others, no matter how obvious or problematic for us, we dwell in a higher self where there is neither judgment nor condemnation.

Similar gifts are available in acknowledging mistakes. A colleague wanted to buy some new speakers for his home stereo system but couldn't afford them. Magically, or so it appeared, he ran into a man outside a music store who offered to sell him some new speakers from the back of a van. My colleague made a few phone calls and satisfied himself that the speakers were not stolen. He then negotiated a good price and made the purchase. The speakers looked great, but when he got them home and hooked them up, he discovered they were of terrible quality.

Mortified with shame, he called his best friend and confessed what an "idiot" he'd been to be scammed by a con artist. His friend told him it was OK to be fallible and that making such a mistake only made him even more lovable. My colleague learned it was OK to make mistakes and to forgive himself for not being perfect. After collecting himself, he mobilized his anger by telephoning the company who sold him the inferior speakers and asked for a full refund. They balked until he informed them he would file a police report because they didn't have a business license in the town where the sale was made. They complied, so he got a valuable lesson about forgiveness at no cost.

It is well known that illness can be a great teacher. Another colleague, a successful psychologist and marathon runner, was diagnosed with cancer and told by his physician he had five years to live. He decided to live his life differently, letting go of his self-admitted arrogance and an ego-based lifestyle. He began meditating, doing Yoga, and walking a spiritual path. He called his illness "God's reset button." This colleague is still alive today, thirty-three years after his diagnosis. He prays daily and is filled with gratitude for the gift of healing. Life is full of situations that seem sad or even tragic, but if we look closely and remain open, we will find hidden gifts and opportunities in every circumstance.

17
Processing Grief Versus Whining

I wonder too…if the rent in the canvas of our life backdrop, the losses that puncture our world, our own emptiness, might actually become places to see.
—Ann Voskamp

God grant me serenity to accept the things I cannot change
Courage to change the things I can
And wisdom to know the difference.

—Reinhold Niebuhr

"Want a little cheese with your whine?" No one likes a whiner, whether it's a demanding child next to you on a cross-country flight or an irritating "grown-up" griping that the salad didn't come with enough croutons (just ask for more). Whining is complaining and often in a tone of voice that others find immature and annoying. In the Twelve Step programs, they talk about "being on the pity pot," a reference to those who fail to move through the stages of grief by holding on to an issue. The expression may sound lacking in empathy, but it is based on the recognition that holding on only perpetuates grief and depression. The point is ultimately that life goes on and we have to resolve grief so we can move forward.

Whining prevents the whiner from finding unexpected gifts in the difficult times or opportunities to learn from stressful life circumstances. Whiners are often blaming or asking, "Why?" Consider an example. You've run into an acquaintance, and this person talks about losing a parent. Sad, indeed, but you meet a year later and your friend shows no sign of "movement" around doing the grief work, "letting go," or moving on. He or she hasn't released the pain through mourning, focused on learning to get support, developed a philosophical/spiritual approach, found gifts like increased compassion, or looked for other opportunities, such as examining his or her own mortality.

Processing is working through an issue by taking certain steps or actions until you reach acceptance or resolution. Acceptance is here defined as consenting and surrendering to what is, which may require saying "yes" to events even if they are painful or unfair. It doesn't mean you have to like what happened or approve of your situation, but you find a way to live with it. This is done by letting go and moving on. Part of the process is to find the gifts and opportunities for learning mentioned (see chapter 21, "Reframing"). This is difficult if not impossible when in the throes of grief, but when you get a little time and distance from the loss, you can begin to look for something positive in what's happened. It's like having a new perspective. As Ann Voskamp suggests in the quote at the start of this chapter, loss and emptiness become places to see more clearly.

As people move through the stages of grieving, they let go of the emotional charge first associated with the loss and free up the energy that had been tied up in emotion. This freed-up energy can appear as you let go of anger, resentment, fear, guilt, sadness, or a sense of unfairness. This will show up as an increase in energy because you are no longer attached to your charged and negative emotions and attitudes. You will be less likely to ruminate and obsess about your loss and thus feel lifted out of depression. Grief is not a bottomless well but a reservoir to be drained!

If, after reading this, you suspect you may have been whining over an unresolved grief issue, take a risk and check it out with a safe friend or family member. Be certain the person you choose is safe before making yourself so vulnerable. The reason for asking is that you don't want to be seen as a whiner or to alienate people around you. Whining contaminates your space and those around you. If you get an affirmative answer and realize you've been whining, ask yourself, "What am I getting out of holding on to my feelings? What am I so afraid of that I can't face this issue and process it through?" Be compassionate with yourself; this just means you haven't had enough support.

If you need help to resolve grief, get it through your church, counseling, Twelve Step program, coaching, mentoring, safe friends or family members, self-help books or tapes and CDs, journaling, or any other productive resource you believe will work for you. There are even certified grief recovery counselors you can find through Grief Recovery Outreach Workshops (GROW) at www.griefrecoverymethod.com. The effort to heal is worth it, as it is too painful to carry burdens that never lighten up.

18
About Forgiveness

It is easy to forgive others, but it didn't occur to me to forgive myself.

—Anonymous

To forgive yourself is the culmination of the healing process and the destination on the journey to self-esteem.

—Stanley Wilson

The process of forgiveness is not a conscious decision, although you can consciously commit to the process of forgiveness. To forgive is not to forget a slight or to develop "celestial amnesia" for abusive behavior. It is not to pretend all is well in order to avoid confrontation with a difficult person. It is not to let people "off the hook" and absolve them of responsibility for harmful behavior. Nor is forgiveness a rationalization that says, "He did the best he could with what he knew at the time." We could forgive Hitler with that logic.

Forgiveness is an artifact, a result of or spinning off from the "letting go" process. The essence of your "letting go" work is that you stop focusing your energy on the interaction of you with the other and learn how to shift your focus to what you need to do for you. This means you let go of a resentment or grievance because to hold on to it will only do you further harm.

Forgiveness cannot be forced. If you try to forgive or let go before you're ready, you get stuck with a laundry list of negative emotions, especially resentment. If you feel like you cannot forgive or let go because of the magnitude of the grievance, you must keep working through the issues until the way out reveals itself to you. If it happens, you will know you have forgiven the person in question or are ready to let go. You may then choose to inform the other person or keep it to yourself. And you don't need to reconcile and reunite with the person who has harmed you. A colleague had a client who forgave her mother for sexually abusing her and then successfully sued her for damages.

My client Laurie told her friend Yolanda that she had started counseling with me. In so doing, she asked Yolanda not to share this with anyone, as it felt personal. Yolanda told Allison, a common friend, and it got back to Laurie, who was justifiably hurt and angry. She told Yolanda she felt betrayed and called her a gossip. Yolanda defended herself by saying it was a slip of the tongue and that it was no big deal anyway. Laurie cut off her friendship with Yolanda and seethed with resentment. She got caught up in a maelstrom of conflicting emotions and began to obsess: "She stabbed me in the back," "She owes me an apology," "Why can't people be trusted?"

At first, Laurie resisted the idea of forgiving or letting go. By holding on to the grievance, she felt validated, and at the same time, she punished Yolanda for her transgression. It also felt self-protective to nurse the grievance, as it protected Laurie from getting hurt and betrayed again. To heal, Laurie had to interrupt her internal dialogue and take the position of healthy advocate to herself. She did this by asking, "What do I want and need for myself in this difficult situation?"

This led to a conversation with Yolanda in which Laurie asked for an apology. Because her anger had cooled and because she was clear in her request, she got the apology and the two reconciled (though Laurie decided to be cautious about making self-disclosures to Yolanda). But even if she hadn't received an apology and even if she did but couldn't forgive her, she could still let go of the grievance by releasing the feelings associated with the transgression.

But what if that which needs to be forgiven is more personal and more conspicuously harmful? In our initial session, Will, an only child, explained how his father had physically abused him for years, while his emotionally unavailable and unprotective mother watched in silence. Like most parents who batter their children, Will's father was aggressive, immature, and lacking in empathy. He, too, had been beaten by his own father and was ignorantly passing along a family legacy. Because he had no interest in hunting and fishing, Will was a constant source of disappointment to his father. Will, handicapped by his father's expectations, had no way to satisfy his father—a setup for abuse. If he forgot to do a chore or didn't do it to his father's specifications or, God-forbid, "talked back," he would be whipped with a belt until welts came up and bled. He came to treatment at age twenty-two feeling humiliated and completely unlovable.

Nonetheless, Will realized he could benefit himself by either forgiving or letting go of his grievances. Over the course of a year, he worked through his painful memories and released his shame and rage. He then wrote a letter to his parents explaining how they had harmed him, how it made him feel about himself, and how he expected to be treated in the future. In sending this letter, Will advocated for the battered child within, reclaimed his power, and set limits on how he would be treated in the future. Predictably, his father blamed Will for the years of abuse ("You made me do it") and his mother said nothing at all in response to the letter. But Will had taken an important step in healing his damaged sense of self by letting go of the emotional baggage he'd been carrying around.

How do you let go of a grievance? The same way you would let go of a shard of broken glass. You drop it because it does you no good to hold on to it. And the way you drop a grievance is to acknowledge it happened, own the feelings associated with it, work them through by expressing those feelings with a safe person, redecide that it was about the person who committed the transgression and not about you, and move on. In so doing, you break the dysfunctional family legacy and carve out a new identity. The alternative to forgiveness is to stay stuck and wounded, in other words, defined by the harmful actions of another person.

To understand everything is to forgive everything.

—Buddha

One cannot forgive without letting go, but one can let go without forgiving.
—Stanley Wilson

19
Sticky Self-Esteem

If you really do put a small value upon yourself, rest assured that the world will not raise your price.

—Anonymous

A man can stand a lot as long as he can stand himself. He can live without hope, without friends, without books, even without music, as long as he can listen to his own thoughts.

—Axel Munthe

Mary, a lonely thirty-six-year-old, arrived at my office with so many issues we never knew which one to land on. In time, we came to realize her struggles boiled down to the feeling of being unworthy of love, undeserving of happiness, and incompetent to deal with life's challenges. This became our focus, as it was an almost perfect definition of low self-esteem.

Mary had been adopted as an infant and was reminded of this almost daily by an unstable mother who taught her she was an emotional and financial burden. As a teen, Mary was teased by her peers for being over-weight and developed a profoundly negative body image. Her mother, rather than supporting Mary, constantly criticized her for being heavy, under the guise of being worried about her health. In relationships with boys and later men, Mary allowed herself to be taken for granted and could never find a voice to assert her own wants and needs.

To add to her problems, she had recently been fired from her job in a college bookstore and decided she was incompetent, despite the fact she'd had seven years of positive evaluations from the same boss who let her go. Here are my process notes from the opening moments of our fourth session.

DL: Do you have a place to start today?

Mary: I've just been really down on myself all week. And I can't seem to pull out of it.

DL: OK. Let's be curious about what you're telling yourself.

Mary: You mean like self-talk?

DL: (nods)

Mary: That I'm fat and ugly. How's that for a start?

DL: Ouch. What happens in your body when you tell me that now?

Mary: (pause) I'm not feeling anything.

DL: Say it again. "I'm fat, and I'm ugly." And pay attention to how your body keeps score.

Mary: I'm fat, and I'm ugly. (pause) I feel kinda sick to my stomach.

DL: Don't move. Just stay with yourself and notice those sensations… the sick feeling in your stomach.

Mary: It hurts.

DL: Say, *I* hurt.

Mary: I hurt. (begins to cry softly)

DL: (hands Mary a box of tissues) This is an old voice. Yes?

Mary: Yes. My mother's voice.

DL: What would you like to have said to your mother? If you could have spoken up for yourself without making matters worse?

Mary: Leave me alone.

DL: Good! But say it like you mean it.

Mary: Leave me alone!

DL: Good! Do you think she's right…That you're fat and ugly?

Mary: No. Not really. I mean, I'm maybe twenty pounds overweight, but that doesn't make me fat.

DL: The problem is you believed her. And now, when you say it to yourself, you still believe it.

Mary: So I should stop saying it?

DL: That'd be nice, but I think you're going to keep hearing it for a while. I think the strategy is to catch yourself parroting your mother and just ask yourself whether or not it's true. It's just an old thought left over from your childhood. That doesn't make it true. It's just a thought.

Mary's story is not an uncommon presentation in therapy. The problem is our minds are programmed to believe what our parents and peers tell us through their reflected appraisals, and too often, these people like to point out our alleged flaws and weaknesses. Maybe it makes them feel better about themselves or maybe they're passing the hot potato of what was done to them, but either way, it's about them. Not us. The antidote is to understand our minds have taken in negative messages and they keep reappearing and perpetuating low self-esteem. We must retrain our minds to notice when this happens and then dispute or detach from the message. In time, we reprogram our brain.

I can imagine some readers thinking, "But I am fat!" OK, maybe you're overweight and need to address the issue. Maybe you're overeating to cope with feelings and it's the actual reason you picked up this book, but it doesn't have to undermine your self-esteem. You wouldn't call a dear friend "fat." You wouldn't call a child "fat," so stop talking to yourself in that way and address it as a health issue. Meanwhile, there is a way to detach from such negative self-talk by observing it rather than automatically reacting to it. There's a big difference between saying, "I'm fat!" without a shred of self-awareness and catching yourself and saying, "My mind is up to its old tricks, telling me I'm fat."

Mary stayed the course for a little more than a year of weekly sessions. In that time, she became more and more aware of how she undermined herself and contributed to her own damaged sense of self-esteem. Eventually, she began to experience a choice. "I can keep talking to myself in this toxic way and suffer the consequences or step back and observe my self-talk without reacting to or believing it." We were able to identify a number of ways she could do repair work, which we jokingly referred to as "self-esteem that sticks." Here are some of those ways:

1. **Practice positive self-talk.** If you are belittling yourself, dispute the message and replace it with positive self-talk. "Well done!" "Great, I did it!" "I deserve respect!" "I'm OK just the way I am!" When Mary told me she was incompetent because of her firing, I asked her to reconcile that belief with her seven years of positive evaluations. Only then did she realize she was fired because she argued with the aging supervisor who failed to grasp the concept of online bookselling.

2. **Accept a compliment.** Fully receive it and take it in. If you were hungry and someone offered you a delicious apple, you wouldn't bat it away. Take it in, and let it nourish you. Mary was actually quite attractive. Whenever I made any mention of how nice she looked, she would automatically deflect the compliment. After I pointed that out a few times, she began to recognize her pattern and take in my complimentary words.

3. **Surround yourself with positive, honest, and healthy people** who support you in your endeavors and in your mistakes. Spend time with them. Avoid abusive, manipulative, or dangerous people. You are as healthy as your environment. Mary eventually found a job at a rival bookstore and worked with a supervisor who treated her with respect. This new position underlined the messages she was by this time giving herself, namely, that she had something positive to offer and was a valued employee. They even supported the practice of online book sales. What a concept!

4. **Take risks that are well researched and based on reality**, so as to set yourself up for success. Accomplishments can boost self-confidence and serve as a springboard toward further successes. When Mary applied for a job at a newer, more progressive bookstore, she

went to her initial interview with the attitude she would be a great addition to the team. The Law of Attraction worked. She got the job.

5. **Practice being a little more patient with yourself and others.** Things take time. Everyone, including you, is entitled to struggle and make mistakes. Mary, who'd failed on every fad diet she'd tried, set a goal of losing one pound a month for a year by exercising every other day and eating more consciously. At the end of a year, she'd actually lost twenty-two pounds.

6. **Accept your feelings and thoughts, all of them.** Allow even those that make you uncomfortable, and remember that you don't have to act on them. You can have opposing thoughts or feelings at the same time. Mary fantasized about telling off the mother who had adopted her and, at first, thought this was evidence that she was an ungrateful daughter and a bad person. In therapy, she willingly embraced her anger and hurt as human and recognized that her mother's toxicity was, in fact, a symptom of mental illness. Unconditional self-acceptance may be the single most important way to improve self-esteem.

7. **Know and monitor your personal limits.** Each of us has limited time, energy, and focus. Mary sometimes worked seventy-hour weeks and then would question why she couldn't get everything done at home. Only when she came to understand the difference between a limitation and a weakness did she lighten up on herself. Even Wonder Woman, the television heroine of the 1970s, had her limitations (her enemies would sometimes steal her belt, sapping her super strength). Wonder Woman could fly; we can't! This is a limitation, not a weakness.

8. **Take responsibility for your life.** You are the captain of your own fate—or at least you could be. Set goals and boundaries that will

honor you as a worthwhile person. Instead of indulging her anger at being fired unjustly, Mary used the anger to motivate her to search for and land a better job. The best revenge *is* success!

9. **Live consciously.** Develop a spiritual or religious belief system that supports you through the difficult times. Mary joined *A Course in Miracles* spiritual study group that reinforced her belief she was a loveable "child of God." Her sense of self-esteem became grounded in what kind of woman she was, as opposed to what size dress she wore.

10. **Exercise regularly.** Exercise clears your head, enhances positive thinking, gives you more energy, and promotes a more positive body image. Mary dedicated herself to working out every other day. She would allow herself to skip a day but never two, and this discipline contributed mightily to her self-confidence.

11. **Act with integrity.** Living in accordance with a personal code of ethics is the foundation of self-esteem. List out and follow steadfastly your most important values, e.g., honesty, respect, loyalty, tolerance, kindness, empathy, service, and so on. Mary really got it that the barometer for her worth was inside her and not dependent on the outside appraisal of a toxic mother or hostile supervisor.

12. **Develop a sense of humor.** Laugh at yourself and situations that come up. Mary actually came in with a wonderful sense of humor. She had only to give herself credit for it. I will never forget her quick wit or infectious laughter.

13. **Forgive yourself.** You are not perfect. It's OK. Be like Mary and let go of your demands for perfection. We all have holes in our socks. Accept this truth, and you'll be well on your way to developing

some sticky self-esteem. I believe it was Goethe, the German writer, who said he could not imagine a crime he did not feel capable of committing. Now, that is acceptance of imperfection!

What would happen if you believed that you are enough?

—Unknown

20
Self-Talk

Tell the negative committee that meets inside your head to sit down and shut up.
—Ann Bradford

My one regret in life is that I am not someone else.

—Woody Allen

Self-talk is pretty much the same as the ideas that occur spontaneously in your mind. I read somewhere that the average person has about sixty thousand thoughts a day, so that's a lot of self-talk. It can be positive, as in "I did a good job on the presentation this morning," or negative as in, "I can't believe I said that to him…What an idiot I am!" Its positivity or negativity is shaped by the persons we have most internalized. If it is influenced by a loving parent or a wise mentor, it is likely to be positive and nurturing. If it repeats messages that came from your abusive stepmother or nasty boyfriend, it will sound negative and toxic. It's actually shocking the way we treat ourselves via self-talk. Much of it is critical, judgmental, and downright mean-spirited, just like the funny but actually sad and profound Woody Allen quote above.

As we develop from children into adults, our self-talk incorporates the words, actions, and nonverbal messages of the people who raised us, whether we admire them, fear them, or hate them. If a shaming parent called you a "bozo" for spilling the milk and parental criticism was a pattern, you may find your self-talk runs along the same self-critical lines. Show me any grown-up whose mind produces an abundance of negative self-talk, and I'll show you someone who feels chronically depressed, powerless, helpless, hopeless, immobilized, and worthless.

The trick is to tune into your self-talk and see if it is positive or negative, toxic or nourishing, critical or compassionate. If you learn how you are attacking yourself with negative self-talk, you will begin to have a choice. You can continue to fire away and maintain your low self-esteem (yes, this is how you maintain low self-esteem) or choose to dispute or detach from your negative self-talk. An example will help illustrate how changing self-talk can be a valuable coping skill.

Felicia is a bright and likable young art student who happens to be about forty pounds over her ideal weight. In one of our first sessions, she alluded to her poor self-image and I asked, "What do you say to yourself when you look in the mirror?"

Her reply was, "That I am disgusting and worthless!"

I followed up with another question, "If you had a dear friend who had the same body type as you, would you tell her she is disgusting and worthless?"

"Of course not," she replied, with a look of horror on her face.

"Then why would you speak to yourself that way?" I asked.

This led to a discussion of how Felicia judged herself in accordance with current cultural values that overvalue slimness and overemphasize looks as a way of determining worth. She decided she no longer wanted to "buy in" to this mind-set, as it left her feeling ashamed and unlovable. Besides, it's just plain wrong!

To change negative self-talk, we must first be aware we're doing it and then either dispute it, detach from it, or both. To pick up on when you're doing it to yourself, be attuned to how it feels to be in your body. For Felicia, this meant noticing how often she felt tense and vaguely ill at ease. Then, she could catch her automatic negative self-talk and replace it with more realistic and constructive words. This is called disputing; for example, instead of "I'm disgusting," she would say, "I need to exercise more and lose some weight, but I accept myself as I am." This technique is a mainstay of Cognitive Behavioral Therapy (CBT) and is backed by research. If she couldn't do this because she truly didn't accept herself, she had the option of detaching. Now she would simply become the observer, the impartial witness who would say, "Oh, my mind is telling me I'm disgusting again. Thanks a lot, mind!" This approach comes from Acceptance and Commitment Therapy (ACT) and is also research-proven. It is accepted in ACT that our minds are not our friends; therefore, we keep an eye on them.

To quicken Felicia's healing, I had her get a three-by-five note card, write out a list of the old negative self-talk, and replace it with new positive self-talk. She was to carry it in her purse and repeat it whenever her self-talk went south, until it became second nature. She also practiced by saying the specific positive self-talk when she looked in a mirror, morning or night. She also posted positive sayings on her mirror, car dashboard, and computer desktop. Once, when Felicia relapsed into telling herself she was disgusting, I said, "You know, we all could exercise a bit more and lose a little weight, but when you talk to yourself that way, <u>it really concerns me</u>." I believe this connecting message helped.

Here are some more examples of Felicia's positive self-talk (predictably, body image was not her only area of self-criticism).

- "I can do this. I'm creative and smart. I've done it before."
- "I can be open to new or positive opportunities."
- "Even though I'm afraid and doubt my abilities, I can do this in small steps and achieve my important goals."
- "I'm a good person and a good catch, and I'll find my true love."
- "I don't need to operate from shame or blame. I am a worthwhile person."
- "Even though it seems like this problem with self-esteem will never end, I know it will."

Self-talk becomes a form of personal counseling when we face stressors, unforeseen difficulties, problems to solve, and new skills to learn, as well as when we need to comfort ourselves. Whenever we face life transitions or challenges, positive self-talk activates healthy coping and mobilizes effective action. This directs our energies and efforts to bring about the most positive direction possible. Think of positive self-talk as rewiring the brain.

Positive self-talk says, "I choose to act rather than react!" This makes positive self-talk the foundation of effective coping, which in turn enables us to achieve our highest form of functioning. We turn our worst adversary into a new best friend!

Self-Talk Worksheet

Old Negative Self-Talk
(notice cues and outcomes)

New Positive Self-Talk
(outcomes)

1._____   1._____

2._____   2._____

3._____   3._____

4._____   4._____

5._____   5._____

6._____   6._____

7._____   7._____

8._____   8._____

9._____   9._____

10._____   10._____

11._____   11._____

12._____   12._____

21
Reframing

Simply stated, *reframing* is a technique whereby we view or think of something or someone in a new and different way; in other words, we change the frame. Whether this technique originated in cognitive psychology, family therapy, or neuro-linguistic programming is less important than the fact that it is very useful in turning negativity into positivity and suffering into happiness.

We all tell ourselves stories and live accordingly. Sometimes, our stories work for us, as in "I'm resilient, and I'm a survivor." Contrast that story to the less constructive, "I'm a victim; I always get the short end of the stick." Narrative therapists tell us these stories say more about our present and future than our past. If my story is that I am a person who perseveres and finds a way to win, I am more likely to win. If I tell myself I'm a loser, I will continue to lose. Look at the story you have authored for your life. Be honest, and then reframe it in a more positive way. Suppose your story is, "I can never find the right job." A new frame would be, "I'm determined to find the right job, and I will."

With reframing, a setback or problem can also be seen as an opportunity. After being cut from her high school volleyball team, my daughter practiced Alexander Graham Bell's saying: "When one door closes, another opens." Looking for other opportunities, she discovered her talent and love for debate. She became the captain of her school debate team, went on to the United States nationals and to a college international debate team, and is now a lawyer. Had she succumbed to the setback of being cut from volleyball, she might never have discovered this other area of life that gave her both pleasure and meaning.

I have a client, Andrea, a twenty-something college student with a penchant for self-criticism and low self-esteem. The other morning, she came in and announced, "I seriously need to slow down. Already today, I went to the Laundromat, got the muffler fixed on my car, gave my dog a bath, and studied for my economics final. And now I'm here!"

I commented, "Wow! I wish I could get that much done in one morning."

Andrea looked dumbstruck. In the frame of negativity, it looked like she was burning herself out. Reframed, it looked like she'd accomplished a great deal and deserved a pat on the back. Indeed, we explored how she felt and she was OK. She wasn't all stressed out, her mood was OK, and she seemed fine. It was just a habit of looking at her experience through a negative lens. The new frame helped Andrea see herself in a new, more positive light, and, more important, it gave her a template for how she could do reframes on her own.

Notice how reframing changes a person's thought process and self-talk in a positive way. It's a new way of looking at things. Life events present an opportunity for learning and preparing for the future. Even loss experiences can be reframed. When you suffer a loss, ask yourself, "What are the potential gifts, the new learning and spiritual growth opportunities, in what's happened?" or "Can I accept this loss and move on in a way that is useful and wise?"

When a loss is fresh and you are in the throes of grief, you may need to wait until the emotional energy is less intense. When the suffering becomes more manageable, be open to the possibility of options. These options are the gifts, lessons, and opportunities for spiritual growth that make us resilient to forces beyond our control (see chapter 16, "Looking for the Gifts and Opportunities"). The willingness to do this empowers us to function at our highest level.

As an example, an old college chum had a below-knee amputation (BKA) from complications of diabetes. When I asked about her adjustment, she said the BKA was "wonderful." She glowed about how she'd gone from being crippled to being independent, from being in excruciating pain to nearly pain free, and from sleeping fitfully to getting a full seven hours a night. Now that's a reframe. "My amputation was wonderful!"

Another type of reframe allows us to be less judgmental and more forgiving. The next time you see someone panhandling or homeless or prostituting or drug addicted and are tempted to think ill of him or her, consider that research tells us these people are way more likely than we to have suffered a high number of "adverse childhood experiences (ACEs)." Indeed, one in twenty adults have had six or more ACEs from a list that includes: physical abuse, sexual abuse, emotional abuse, neglect, a mentally ill person in the home, an alcoholic or drug addict family member, witnessing violence to the mother, loss of a parent via abandonment or death, or an incarcerated parent. Many of us have experienced two or three of these, but imagine having six or more! These experiences accumulate and affect brain development, and such persons have far less of a chance to succeed in life.

Instead of a judgment, the proper reframe becomes, "That brother or sister looks like he or she is carrying a heavy burden." You are separate from what you think. You can retrain your brain to use reframes and live a more constructive, productive life.

We shape clay into a pot
But it is the emptiness inside
That holds whatever we want.
—Tao Te Ching

Reframing Worksheet

Event/Situation	Present Frame (Self-Talk)	Reframe (Self-Talk)
1. _____ _____ _____	_____ _____ _____	_____ _____ _____
2. _____ _____ _____	_____ _____ _____	_____ _____ _____
3. _____ _____ _____	_____ _____ _____	_____ _____ _____
4. _____ _____ _____	_____ _____ _____	_____ _____ _____
5. _____ _____ _____	_____ _____ _____	_____ _____ _____
6. _____ _____ _____	_____ _____ _____	_____ _____ _____
7. _____ _____ _____	_____ _____ _____	_____ _____ _____

22
Don't Lose Yourself in the "Theys"

But it's all right now, I learned my lesson well.
You see, ya can't please everyone, so ya got to please yourself.

—Ricky Nelson

In 1952, when I was a young girl, eleven-year-old Ricky Nelson joined *The Adventures of Ozzie and Harriet*, his parents' family-friendly television sitcom. Within five years, Ricky became a teenage heartthrob and rock-'n'-roll star, with a number of big hits. His star faded in the midsixties, but in 1971, he was invited to play in a reunion show at Madison Square Garden. By this time, Ricky had crossed over to country rock, and when he tried to play his new material, he was virtually booed off the stage. Shaken, he wrote a song about this experience, and ironically, it became his biggest hit, "Garden Party." The chorus is the topic of this chapter ("But it's all right now, I learned my lesson well. You see, ya can't please everyone, so ya got to please yourself"). Ricky learned to be true to himself and not lose himself in the "theys."

Many of us are afraid to do what we really want to do for fear of what the "theys" might think or of what they might say to us or about us. We abandon our dreams for fear of being judged, as if someone else has all the answers or knows what's best for us. Consider the following example. Linda wanted to open an espresso stand in the parking lot of a large grocery store. There were no espresso stands within a mile in Linda's coffee-obsessed area of the Pacific Northwest. She negotiated a favorable lease with the grocery store and began looking into what kind of franchise would be most profitable. But then she lost herself in the "theys." Her banker and even her husband told her it would be financial suicide to try to start a business when she had no business experience. Linda began to doubt herself, gave up the idea, and settled into a deep depression. A few months later, an espresso stand opened in her exact location and was wildly successful.

Who are the "theys" anyway? They could be just about anybody—a controlling spouse, an internalized parent, a real-life parent, your best friend, the next-door neighbor, a self-righteous minister, an audience, or people in general. Keep in mind we define our identities by acknowledging and expressing our true feelings, needs, desires, and opinions. People carve out an identity when they make statements like "I'm joining an antiwar group," or "I've decided to go back to college," or "I want to write a book." When we abandon such dreams because others might disapprove or argue against us, we lose ourselves in the "theys." We, in effect, give away our power, abandon our true self, and settle for a false one. Don't be that person!

An old story makes the point. An elderly grandfather sets out with his young grandson to go to the market. With them is the old man's donkey. Grandfather places the boy on the donkey's back, and off they go. Soon, they pass travelers headed in the opposite direction. One looks over and comments, in a derisive tone, "Will you look at that? That thoughtless boy makes the old man walk on a hot day!" Grandfather and Grandson hear the comment and decide it would be best to trade places. They continue on, and soon they encounter more travelers. This time, they hear the comment, "Will you look at that? That thoughtless old man makes the little boy walk on a hot day!" Bewildered, they decide to both walk and avoid any further criticism. Soon, another traveler looks over and says, "Will you look at that? A perfectly good beast of burden and neither of them have the good sense to ride it on a hot day!" Again, they stop, and this time, they decide to both ride the donkey. It isn't long before they pass more travelers, and sure enough, one comments, "Will you look at that? How inconsiderate of them to both ride that animal on such a hot day!" Get the point?

If you're invested in pleasing the "theys," you will never get it right. There's nothing wrong with wanting or even seeking approval, but when it means selling yourself down the river, you've lost yourself in the "theys." This doesn't mean you can't listen to feedback from others or factor others' ideas into your decision-making, but, in the end, you must learn to follow your own heart to be truly you. The truth is most people are so busy and focused on their own lives that they aren't paying real attention to what you are doing, anyway. The visionaries of the world have introduced change precisely because they were willing to follow their dreams and tune out the naysayer "theys." Be a visionary. Be the agent of your own experience.

I Choose…

To live by choice, not by chance;
To make changes, not excuses;
To be motivated, not manipulated;
To be useful, not used;
To excel, not compete.
I choose self-esteem, not self-pity.
I choose to listen to my inner voice,
Not the random opinions of others.

—Unknown

Don't Lose Yourself in the "Theys" Worksheet

If we are always guided by other people's thoughts, what is the point of having our own?

—Oscar Wilde

Pay attention to your thoughts, and catch yourself worrying about the disapproving "theys." If you're tempted to negate yourself for fear of what someone else might think or say, consider the moment as an opportunity for self-actualization and personal growth. Then, focus in on your situation and notice how giving away your power feels in your body. Do you feel anxious or fearful? Do you experience a tight or uncomfortable sensation in your gut? Be aware that you're wrestling with the "theys," and make a commitment to be true to yourself. Face the fear no matter how scary or unfamiliar it feels to hold your ground. Support yourself with some positive self-talk along the lines of, "I'm a grown-up. I refuse to give my power to anyone else." Or have a chuckle and remember Ricky's lyrics: "*You see, ya can't please everyone, so ya got to please yourself.*"

Practice by listing some situations where you are worried about what others will think of you, and then keep track of bodily cues that inform you that you're about to make a mistake. Finally, write out the appropriate self-talk that will ensure you don't lose yourself in the "theys."

	<u>Situation</u>	<u>Emotional/Bodily Cues</u>	<u>Self-Talk</u>
1.	_____	_____	_____
2.	_____	_____	_____

3. _____ _____ _____

4. _____ _____ _____

5. _____ _____ _____

6. _____ _____ _____

7. _____ _____ _____

8. _____ _____ _____

9. _____ _____ _____

10. _____ _____ _____

Do It Anyway

People are often unreasonable, illogical, and self-centered;
Forgive them anyway.

If you are kind, people may accuse you of selfish, ulterior motives;
Be kind anyway.

If you are successful you will win some false friends and true enemies;
Succeed anyway.

If you are honest and frank, people may cheat you;
Be honest and frank anyway.

What you spend years building, someone could destroy overnight;
Build anyway.

If you find serenity and happiness, they may be jealous;
Be happy anyway.

The good you do today, people will often forget tomorrow;
Do good anyway.

Give the world the best you have, and it may never be enough;
Give the world the best you've got anyway.

You see, in the final analysis, it is between you and God;
It was never between you and them anyway.

—Kent Keith

23
Never Be a Victim Again

Don't volunteer to be a victim.

—Unknown

This above all, to refuse to be a victim.

—Margaret Atwood

That night was an especially exciting one for fifteen-year-old Bridget. She had only just met Brandon, but he'd offered to pick her up at the south entrance to the mall and take her to a party in North Seattle. At seventeen, he could drive, an incentive that gave Bridget a little thrill in and of itself. She arrived early and waited at the curb outside the food court, by herself, thinking about Brandon.

For reasons she didn't quite understand, Bridget felt apprehensive about this boy. Maybe because he seemed a little too cool and full of himself when they met at the skateboard park. Maybe because he was on suspension from high school for getting caught with a pint of vodka in his backpack. But she decided it was silly to think there was anything wrong with Brandon, everyone she knew experimented with alcohol, and besides, the girl who had introduced her to him said he was OK. She told herself to stop worrying. Worrying was what her mother did. Always thinking about how dangerous it was to be a teenage girl nowadays.

By the time Brandon arrived, twenty minutes late, Bridget had begun to wonder if she should get back on the bus and head home. She was about to leave when a pickup truck with fancy chrome wheels sped up to the curb and stopped abruptly. The passenger door flew open. Inside, the boy she'd met once grinned invitingly. Bridget climbed in, and off they went, Brandon apologizing for being late. He seemed sincere, yet there was something that sounded wrong in his voice or perhaps that was just her imagination. They drove to a residential area in Seattle and got themselves a bit lost, though that seemed weird too, because Brandon drove as if he knew exactly where he was going. Bridget told herself her mind was playing tricks on her, this driving with a boy and going to a party being so new and exciting.

When Brandon finally found the place, an expensive home in a nice neighborhood, they exited his truck and began walking up a flight of steps to the front door. That Brandon walked ahead of her and too fast annoyed her, and he appeared to be looking from side to side to see if anyone was watching. "Oh well, that makes sense," Bridget reasoned. Teen parties rarely have parental approval and he probably wanted to make sure they were arriving under the radar.

A clean-cut-looking boy about her age or a little older opened the door and invited them in. There were four boys and only one other girl. That made Bridget a little uncomfortable, but after introductions were made, she felt better. Besides, Brandon was paying close attention to her so she allowed herself to relax. Then she relaxed even more with a glass of red wine. She told herself not to have more than two because she didn't want to get drunk, but this wine seemed really strong and before she knew it, she felt woozy. Fortunately, Brandon led her down the stairs and into the basement where she could lie down for a while. He seemed so kind and concerned. She let him lie next to her on the bed because he promised not to touch her even if she passed out. But he broke his promise.

Bridget came to me at age eighteen, two years after the rape. For two of those years, she'd used the drug ecstasy on an almost daily basis in a failed attempt to erase the memory of what had happened. By staying high, she avoided the maelstrom of negative feelings associated with such a horrific experience. I asked if she'd told anyone else what had happened and was not surprised when she answered, "No." She blamed herself for Brandon's criminal behavior and directed her rage at him back on herself. Only when I told her she'd been slipped a date rape drug did she begin to forgive herself for ending up isolated with a sexual predator.

Sadly, in the years between the rape and therapy, Bridget continued to put herself in dangerous situations. Therapists refer to this as "trauma reenactment." As is the case with many victims of rape, she felt undeserving of safety and unworthy of love. Troubled and suffering low self-esteem, she continued to date "bad boys" and was date-raped on two more occasions after drinking too much. Not surprisingly, Bridget's presenting problems were the anxiety that comes with post-traumatic stress disorder and guilt over her sexual behavior. Fear permeated every aspect of her life, yet she continued to engage in high-risk behavior. Unless she could take better care of herself, the therapy wasn't going to work because she kept getting retraumatized. That made the first order of business with Bridget to teach her to stay out of harm's way. We adopted the following strategies:

1. **Pick safe people and safe places.** You deserve safety in every circumstance. If there is any question about a person or place, don't allow yourself to be compromised. Bridget agreed to give up the party life and avoid frequenting places where young people met to do drugs. Over time, she developed a new group of friends.

2. **Red flag the obvious.** Red flag any and all behaviors that make you feel anxious or uncomfortable. Confront the source of your discomfort, and state clearly how you expect to be treated. Bridget went on three dates with a young man who refused to disclose what he did for a living. She liked him but let him know his secretiveness made her nervous. When he refused to open up, she ended the relationship.

3. **Learn to say, "NO!"** It is your right to assert yourself forcefully in any situation you suspect might lead to harm. This is how you reclaim your power. Bridget was enjoying a conversation with a young man who lived in the same apartment complex. When he pressured her to go up to his unit so he could show off his Sony PlayStation, Bridget got an uncomfortable sensation in her stomach

and refused. She simply said, "No," and when he acted offended, she left the pool area where they'd been conversing.

4. **Know your boundaries, and express them clearly.** We are safe within our boundaries, so if you are unaware of yours, discover them. It may sound cliché, but people usually do treat us the way we train them to. Even during treatment, Bridget had a difficult time setting limits. She met a young man who attended a college almost two hours away. They hit it off so she was willing to drive up to see him, but whenever she asked him to reciprocate, he always had an excuse. Unwisely, she gave in by always being the one to travel. Her resentment grew, and the relationship ended badly.

5. **Consider your choices.** Look for and consider all the choices available to you, rather than assuming you don't have any. Ask yourself, "How can I best respond to this person?" "What are my options in this situation?" One choice Bridget had not considered was to take some time off from dating to clarify her values and decide what she really wanted from life. When she did, she found an inner strength and an ability to be good company to herself she did not know existed.

6. **Reframe the way you look at things.** The same picture can look better in a new frame. Accept the fact that life is often unfair, grieve your losses, and move on. Bridget dropped the image of herself as a victim and instead chose to see herself as a survivor, able to extend heartfelt compassion and wisdom to others—and to herself!

7. **Pick a healthy support system, and put them to use.** If a red flag goes up, get the opinion of a trusted friend, family member, professional, minister, or Twelve Step group. Able to develop a trusting relationship with me, Bridget openly discussed her most vulnerable feelings. On occasion and with my encouragement, she would telephone me in between sessions for help with an immediate

problem. This represented a huge gain, as she had unsuccessfully "licked her own wounds" her entire life. Asking for help was a "new story."

8. **Practice good decision-making skills.** Without good decision-making skills, you may very well put yourself in compromising situations. With Bridget, we used a "stop-and-pause" strategy before she made any decision that involved relating to the young men she attracted. During the pause, she would consider her thoughts, feelings, and intuitions before proceeding.

9. **Collect information based on reality.** Get your facts straight. If you have to make decisions or take a risk, make sure your resources are factual. One of Bridget's most important lessons was to acknowledge, "Some men can be trusted." This required her to make decisions based on fact rather than overgeneralization.

10. **Use your front-end and back-end skills.** If you can't say or do what you want on the spot, think it over and decide if you want to come back and say or do something later. Such back-end work empowers you and increases your choices. As I told Bridget, "It's easier to answer the quiz show questions when you're at home," so don't be afraid to say, "I need some time to mull that over. I'll get back to you tomorrow."

11. **Give up your perfectionism.** Sometimes, we're so busy making sure others don't victimize us, we forget we can victimize ourselves. Learn to give it your best shot and then walk away or let go. For a while, Bridget did a one-eighty and sought the "perfect" boyfriend. He had to be trustworthy, respectful, supportive, ambitious, funny, cute, and a good dancer. Eventually, she realized there are no perfect men (note: or women) and became willing to accept a young man who had most of the qualities she sought. Aim high, but be realistic.

12. **Remember privacy and control.** Victimizers need privacy to control you and act out their bad intentions. Don't go anywhere alone with someone who hasn't yet earned your trust. This important rule would have saved Bridget from being drugged and date-raped. That is not to blame her but to emphasize this crucial strategy.

As children, many of us become victims because we are naïve and have no power. We are easy prey to the abusers and predators of the world. As adults, it is imperative we cease to see ourselves as victims, even if, like Bridget, we were tricked and exploited in the worst possible ways. When you define yourself as a victim, you forfeit your power and strength, leaving you vulnerable to the possibility of reenacting trauma scenes from childhood. This will almost certainly guarantee more traumatic experiences and more suffering.

In adopting the above strategies, the courageous Bridget redefined herself as a survivor, a young woman to be reckoned with. She is currently dating a college classmate who treats her with consideration and respect. He can be clingy and demanding at times, but she does well in setting limits with him. They enjoy one another's company and have a lot of fun together. She continues to struggle but struggles successfully in the sense that she no longer makes herself a victim.

24
Checking in with Yourself (Managing Emotional Triggers)

One cannot reflect in streaming water. Only those who know internal peace can give it to others.

—Lao Tzu

When you don't know what to do, get still. The answer will come.

—Oprah Winfrey

Bob Dylan, in his bizarre midsixties "*Ballad of a Thin Man*" belts out the line, "*Because something is happening here and you don't know what it is...do you, Mr. Jones?*" The iconic songwriter has touched upon a common and painful dilemma for many of us. We are aware that something is happening in our mind and body, possibly something important about who we are or what we need to do, but we haven't a clue as to whether it's a body sensation, a feeling, a thought, an image, or some combination of the above. We are so bombarded by life experience that it's hard to sort it out.

Let's say we actually know it's a feeling; we might still be unsure whether it's frustration, jealousy, envy, aggression, rage, or some other emotion. And what if we're actually certain it is jealousy, what then would be the skillful and effective way to deal with it? Should we share this feeling and risk embarrassment or alienation or squelch it and suffer the consequences of blocking emotions in our bodies. No wonder we get so backed up with so much of what enters our awareness. No wonder we can't figure ourselves out and act accordingly without internal conflict.

I want to make a case for using self-awareness to keep our registers clear. Awareness gives us a menu of choices in every situation. For instance, feelings are like arrows, directing us to take the right or appropriate action. If we're frightened, we can get to a place of safety. If we're angry, we can tell someone to back off or change their behavior. If we're filled with joy, we can smile and hug a friend. If we're grieving, we cry, mourn, and seek the loving support of others.

Feelings are often preceded by thoughts, body sensations, and images. If I think my close friend is treating me unfairly, I notice my body tenses and I get an image of telling her off. This is how I know I am more than likely hurt and angry. This directs me to express my feelings to my friend in a way that lets her know my experience and also to stop doing what she did that was hurtful. This is what I mean by keeping the register clear. Feelings that go unnoticed and unexpressed have a way of ending up frozen in the musculature as blocked energy. Because the body keeps score, we are prone to developing physical symptoms that are really manifestations of the unexpressed emotions.

Here are ten ways to live a more conscious life, one where self-awareness guides us to say what's so and do so in a way that is more likely to get us what we want. These activities make clear what we have on the register and therefore allow us a choice to express ourselves.

1. **Meditation.** A great way to relax and to get centered so we can explore what is just beyond our conscious awareness. Through meditation, we go deeper and balance what is reactive within us.

2. **Yoga, Tai Chi, and Qi Gong**. Energy exercises that locate the knots in your body and release tension. They are like acupressure treatments but without the needles.

3. **Exercise**. Allows you to let go of the inevitable stress of life while clearing your mind so you can focus on what's bothering you. It is a known mood enhancer.

4. **Cultural Outlets.** The Native American tradition of burning sage, cedar, and sweetgrass can open the mind and body to whatever is

going on inside. The same is true for burning incense or candles or cooking traditional foods.

5. **Using a Ritual**. A series of ceremonial actions that can emotionally calm you and allow access to deeper levels. A list of my favorites would include taking a warm bath, burning candles, communing with nature, gardening, reading, sitting in a rocking chair, drinking a nice cup of tea, or petting a dog or cat.

6. **Journaling.** Writing about your experience, not only accesses feelings, but allows you to process and use them. Ask yourself what part of you knows about any troublesome issues. Don't censure or censor what comes up; instead, stay open until the answer bubbles into awareness. Then, "write the wrong" to unburden yourself from negative feelings and attitudes.

7. **Listening to or playing music.** This will put you in a reflective place to "check in" on present thoughts, emotions, and body sensations. Classical or New Age music is especially conducive to enhanced awareness. And it also gets emotions moving.

8. **Attending church.** The safety and support of a communal experience, centers you spiritually and promotes self-exploration. Church is often a good place to find a sympathetic ear.

9. **Counseling or psychotherapy.** The goal of most individual and group therapy, is to help you reconnect with yourself so you can live a happier, more meaningful life. There is also an emphasis on healthy self-expression.

10. **Attending Twelve Step meetings.** Get the support and structure you need to avoid any and all substances that alter awareness. Hear the stories of others, and share your own.

Checking in with Yourself (Managing Emotional Triggers) Worksheet

Helpful questions to ask when triggered:

1. What is going on, physically or emotionally?

_____

_____

_____

2. It seems like I am stressed/upset/angry/anxious/grieving; what could it be?

_____

_____

_____

3. When did these feelings start?

_____

_____

_____

4. What was happening at that time?

_____

_____

_____

5. What were the events that triggered me?

_____

_____

_____

6. Is it real or not?

_____

_____

_____

7. Is it my problem or someone else's?

_____

_____

_____

8. What is within my control?

_____

_____

_____

9. What isn't within my control?

_____

_____

_____

10. What are my options in dealing with this triggering (using self-talk; talking to safe, supportive people; journaling; collecting information based on reality; allowing myself to grieve; problem-solving; nurturing myself; and so on)?

_____

_____

_____

Common Emotional Triggers Worksheet

Triggers Past and Present	Cues Physical/Emotional	What to Do and What to Say
1. _____	_____	_____
_____	_____	_____
_____	_____	_____
_____	_____	_____
_____	_____	_____
_____	_____	_____
2. _____	_____	_____
_____	_____	_____
_____	_____	_____
_____	_____	_____
_____	_____	_____
_____	_____	_____
3. _____	_____	_____
_____	_____	_____
_____	_____	_____
_____	_____	_____
_____	_____	_____
_____	_____	_____
4. _____	_____	_____
_____	_____	_____
_____	_____	_____
_____	_____	_____
_____	_____	_____

Know that you have a center. Know that you belong there. Know that the path to the center takes no effort.

—Deepak Chopra

Who can wait quietly until the mud settles? Who can remain still until the moment of action?

—Lao Tzu

25
The Difference between Intuition and Triggering

Intuition will tell the thinking mind where to look next.

—Jonas Salk

Your intuition will tell you where you need to go; it will connect you with people you should meet; it will guide you toward work that is meaningful for you—work that brings you joy, work that feels right for you.

—Shakti Gawain

We have previously defined intuition as a form of knowing that comes without conscious reasoning This makes it sound like a magical phenomenon, but, in fact, it's quite the opposite; it's something wired into the body and brain of humans for survival purposes, like an instinct. Consider the statement of one of my clients: "Something was very wrong with this guy. I couldn't put my finger on what it was, but I knew he was off and off in a bad way." Here, my client is using her intuition to guide her to stay out of harm's way. This is an excellent use of one's intuitive abilities.

Intuition should not be confused with triggering. I define triggering as a reaction to a situation, event, or person that is greater than what the situation calls for. In simple terms, it is an overreaction that is more intense or forcible than justified. Another client, call her Tiffany, became triggered when a man she barely knew put his arm around her in a bar. He touched her so she bloodied his nose. Tiffany had been sexually assaulted several months before this happened, and her feelings were raw. While it was inappropriate for the man to touch her without her consent, it was an overreaction for her to assault him for what amounted to a minor offense.

Sometimes triggering is similar to what psychologists call transference. In transference, emotions that typically originate in childhood are transferred or redirected to a substitute person who reminds us of another. Say you grew up with a controlling stepmother who favored her own daughter and made you do extra chores. If you subsequently had a female college professor with a high need for control, the anger you would ordinarily feel for her becomes amplified as you transfer old feelings from the past. If the professor then showed favoritism toward a "pet" female student and assigned you extra homework, you might be unconsciously triggered and react in a way that is way out of proportion to the situation at hand.

Tiffany, after learning about the difference between intuition and triggering, defined a trigger as the one that left a "bad aftertaste" in her mouth. On some level, she knew she had overreacted to the man she assaulted and had to step back from the situation to get some distance and perspective. When triggered but not aware of it, she would get stuck in anger, sadness, fear, shame, or defensiveness. With awareness, she was able to take responsibility and let the feeling go. She had the "bad aftertaste" with regard to the man in the bar and avoided legal consequences by sincerely apologizing. Fortunately for both, the man did not need medical attention and may also have realized it is not good form to be touching women he didn't know. As you would imagine, almost all violent act-outs involve some aspect of triggering.

The worksheet to follow will help you differentiate between intuition and triggering. Whereas intuition is the wise knowing that comes from a centered place within, triggering involves more emotional arousal and intense bodily sensation. By paying attention to physical and emotional cues, you should be able to tell one from the other and respond appropriately. If it is triggering, ask yourself, "What does this situation remind me of from the past (father, brother, teacher, and so on)?" Say to yourself, "This is not the past. What can I do to respond to this situation accordingly? Do I need to take a break and come back or just disengage entirely?" If you are having trouble managing yourself because of triggering, seek professional help.

Intuition and Triggering Worksheet

Situation	Intuition or Triggering	Physical/ Emotional Cues	Self-Talk
1._____	_____	_____	_____
2._____	_____	_____	_____
3._____	_____	_____	_____
4._____	_____	_____	_____
5._____	_____	_____	_____
6._____	_____	_____	_____
7._____	_____	_____	_____
8._____	_____	_____	_____
9._____	_____	_____	_____
10._____	_____	_____	_____
11._____	_____	_____	_____
12._____	_____	_____	_____

26
Probing Your Intuition

Intuition is always right in at least two important ways;
It is always in response to something.
It always has your best interest at heart.

—Gavin de Becker

Intuition is a spiritual faculty and does not explain, but simply points the
way.

—Florence Scovel Shinn

The only time your intuition doesn't work is when you ignore it. This is because intuition is wired into our brains and bodies as a survival tool. It is the ability to understand a situation or person instinctively and instantly, without conscious deliberation. In other words, it's the "gut feeling" we get when we know something but are not relying on either observation or reason.

Everyone is intuitive, as it is wired into all humans for survival purposes. It is the "Wise Part" of you that has a "hunch" about a particular person or situation. It is that little voice inside that tells you the best way to deal with someone or the wise thing to do. For example, your intuition may tell you, "Take your time," "Get a closer look," "Don't get a closer look," "He gives me the creeps," "She seems like bad news," "Get away from that person," or "Collect more information based on reality." When you hear these kinds of messages from that voice in your head, stop, look, and listen!

Many people are good at using their intuition in giving advice to others, but ignore their own inner counsel. My friend, call her Sylvia, is a bright and successful professional woman who has an excellent track record of advising friends and clients on financial matters. At a lunch meeting, she shared that she had a new boyfriend and was excited about their long-term prospects. When she told me about Ron, I could sense something wasn't quite right (my own intuition) about their new relationship. I asked her if she had any gut instincts about him that she might be overlooking. She hesitated a few moments and told me the first time they met, she got a bad vibe from him, that he might be a sex addict, but she dismissed it and convinced herself she was being overly critical. They'd dated for nearly two months, and her intuition had not proven out. I suggested that she proceed with caution. I received a phone call from a distraught Sylvia a couple weeks after that. Indeed, her first take was the correct one. Ron was sleazy. While taking a photo with his smartphone, she hit the wrong button and found saved pictures of naked women (who turned out to be former girlfriends).

Intuition isn't 100 percent effective, but it's uncanny how often these first hunches are. Pay close attention to them if you wish to make wise decisions and protect yourself (see chapter 25, "The Difference between Intuition and Triggering").

Like Sylvia, many times we say we don't trust ourselves or our decisions. In the beginning, we knew what our intuition was trying to tell us but sort of tuned out our "gut." We overrode our instincts and behaved foolishly and impulsively. I believe the best way to make great decisions, to protect ourselves and secure good relationships, is to slow down and check in with our intuitive self. This means listening to our "Wise Part," honoring hunches, and collecting information while operating in reality. Use the following worksheet to make this happen.

By the way, if you're wondering why I keep harping on the subject of listening to your intuition, it is because it is a crucial coping skill.

Let yourself be silently drawn,
By the strange pull of what you really love.
It will not lead you astray.

—Rumi

Probing Your Intuition Worksheet

	Situation	Listening/Not Listening	Duration of Slip
1.	_____	_____	_____
	_____	_____	_____
	_____	_____	_____
2.	_____	_____	_____
	_____	_____	_____
	_____	_____	_____
3.	_____	_____	_____
	_____	_____	_____
	_____	_____	_____
4.	_____	_____	_____
	_____	_____	_____
	_____	_____	_____
5.	_____	_____	_____
	_____	_____	_____
	_____	_____	_____
6.	_____	_____	_____
	_____	_____	_____
	_____	_____	_____
7.	_____	_____	_____
	_____	_____	_____
	_____	_____	_____

27
Do Your Passions Match Up with Your Personal Values?

It is with our passions as it is with fire and water. They are good servants, but bad masters.

—Roger L'Estrange

The happiness of a man in this life does not consist in the absence, but in the mastery of his passions.

—Alfred Lord Tennyson

Passion, in the sense I am using it, means a strong desire or enthusiasm for something, such as a belief, behavior, activity, hobby, or cause. Some people are passionate about their faith, some about vegetarian cooking, some about surfing in Hawaii, some about their favorite sports team, and some about volunteering to help the homeless.

Healthy passion generates an enthusiasm for life and reflects one's most cherished values. Unhealthy passion does neither. Its energy comes from tension, and this makes it more like an act-out, an attempt to resolve some emotional issue without any consciousness. As such, it can be self-defeating and downright dangerous.

Feeling passionate about something often goes hand in hand with your values. While an entire book could be devoted to this topic, I will simply say values are what you consider most important in the way you live your life. Life goes better when we identify our values and honor them accordingly. If you value beauty in nature but rarely venture outside, your life will be neither fulfilling nor happy. If your highest value is social justice and you volunteer for Habitat for Humanity and donate a part of your income to Amnesty International, you will derive great satisfaction from your efforts. Get behind your values if you want to be happier.

I've worked with any number of women whose highest value was creativity, yet they'd lapsed into boredom and depression because they were creating nothing. Once they started writing, painting, sculpting, scrapbooking, photographing, making stained glass or jewelry, and so on, their moods lifted dramatically and life seemed full of zest, spirituality, and gratification. Once we clarify our cherished values, they will guide our decisions and keep us moving in the right direction.

Let's return to the differences between healthy and unhealthy passion. Healthy passion feels good and is aligned with the values you hold dear. It is energizing over the long run and free of self-doubt or conflict. It feels quieter, calmer, more centered, and more satisfying as you engage in whatever it is that has passion around it. It is energizing over the long run and feels right because it aligns with your priorities. If you follow your healthy passions and come from your spiritual center, you will experience more freedom and happiness.

Unhealthy passion is also charged with energy, but typically it becomes obsessive or addictive. This kind of passion is often fueled by fear and can easily morph into manic behavior. Think of people you've known who are passionate about exercise, but they lose perspective and it becomes a compulsive act. When this happens, unhealthy passion actually becomes contradictory to your values because you started out wanting to be healthier. Such behavior will not free you up; in fact, doing it may lead to behavior that is against your conscious wishes. You will be drained or find yourself in trouble. At its worst, an unhealthy passion will tear at your self-esteem and end up in shame and regret. When passion gone wrong leads to a loss of control and an abandonment of your values, it can negatively affect your job, family, and friends.

Natalie, an attractive woman in her late thirties, came to therapy for an issue unrelated to her unhealthy passion. She reminded me of a sixties hippie, with her unconventional appearance and free-spirit lifestyle. It was a specific problem that brought her, a conflict in the workplace related to the way she dressed. A middle school teacher, she often wore low-cut blouses that showed cleavage and she sometimes went braless. Her principal and vice principal had reprimanded her, but to no avail. The school had no dress code for teachers, so Natalie stubbornly told them to mind their own business. Eventually, faced with the threat of losing her job, she consented to attend six sessions to deal with what her bosses called poor boundaries and willful disobedience.

Rather than lecture Natalie about her position as a role model, I heard her say she should set an example for the young girls she taught and avoid objectifying herself in front of young boys. This way, the idea came from her and she didn't feel controlled, as she did when school authority figures told her how to dress. She could still honor her value of being independent and different, but without doing it in a way that might harm her students.

Once the presenting issue was settled, I learned that Natalie was a risk taker and thrill seeker. "I have a passion for adventure," she exclaimed, and she lit up like a Christmas tree when she said it. In particular, I found out that she would regularly hitchhike on weekends, especially into the mountains where she would then walk remote trails alone. Miraculously, she had never been assaulted, though she admitted to a very scary situation with a male driver who propositioned her and then got angry when she asked to be let out of the car.

I confronted Natalie by telling her I considered this an unhealthy passion and that I was more than a little concerned for her safety. I asked her to consider staying on for more than the six sessions she'd agreed to, and she consented. She told me that hitchhiking made her feel "alive," and that she had been doing it since leaving home at age seventeen.

After one of her adventures, Natalie would acknowledge a vague sense of unease, especially in her gut, which I interpreted as the wisdom of the body. Her intuition and her stomach were telling her she was doing something that put herself in harm's way. I still see Natalie, and, not surprisingly, we have discovered that her passion for adventure is a way of jacking up her excitement levels. This is really a defense, a way of avoiding chronic feelings of emptiness, loneliness, and boredom.

Moreover, Natalie's risk-taking is related to an unresolved trauma as a teen, namely, her alcoholic stepfather would touch her inappropriately and then claim it was accidental. By taking chances where someone could end up molesting her, she unconsciously put herself in a situation where she reenacted her trauma history. Perhaps this was unconsciously a way to try to work it out, but it had nothing to do with a healthy passion for adventure.

Therapy for Natalie is working, though slowly. We are currently in her third year of treatment. She no longer hitchhikes and is now aware that she was fortunate to behave so recklessly for so long without consequences. She now tries to get her excitement from hiking responsibly, skydiving, scuba diving, river rafting, downhill skiing, and other outdoor activities. There never was any problem per se with her "passion for adventure," but she was acting it out in an unhealthy way by taking an unnecessary and immature risk.

Now we have Natalie examine different situations and activities, how she feels before and after engaging in them, and then decide accordingly whether they are healthy or unhealthy. She also looks at how her activities align with her core values, having realized that she is happiest and proudest of herself when she does things that involve healthy risk-taking.

The following worksheet helped Natalie to be aware of what she was doing and gave her the wherewithal to make better decisions. She has decided to pursue only healthy passions, as they are sufficient to keep her out of boredom and depression. And because they align with her valuing adventure, she feels happy and fulfilled.

What kind of passion do you have?

Do Your Passions Match Up with Your Personal Values? Worksheet

How Does This Activity Make You Feel?

Situation	Before	After
1. _____	_____	_____
2. _____	_____	_____
3. _____	_____	_____
4. _____	_____	_____
5. _____	_____	_____
6. _____	_____	_____
7. _____	_____	_____
8. _____	_____	_____
9. _____	_____	_____

Does the above situation match up with your values, safety, and health?

Core Value	Safety	Healthy	Unhealthy
1. _____	_____	_____	_____
2. _____	_____	_____	_____
3. _____	_____	_____	_____
4. _____	_____	_____	_____
5. _____	_____	_____	_____
6. _____	_____	_____	_____
7. _____	_____	_____	_____
8. _____	_____	_____	_____
9. _____	_____	_____	_____

28
Me...and My Shadow
(Who Is the Observer?)

There are two distinct aspects of your inner being. The first is you, the awareness, the witness, the center of your willful intentions; and the other is that which you watch.

—Michael A. Singer

There is in all of us an "observer." You could call it the seat of consciousness or a center of awareness, but it is really the part of us that watches our experience. When we are aware that we are aware and aware of what we are aware of, we have taken a giant step toward being a true spiritual being. The alternative is ignorance, to live in a world of knee-jerk reactivity and unconscious behavior. Instead of being hopelessly lost in the movie of your life, you can watch the movie without getting caught up in all the drama.

All the great religions have identified this place of higher consciousness. In Judeo-Christian teachings, it is known as the Soul; in Buddhism, it is the Self; in Hinduism, it is the Atman; and in metaphysics, it is the Spirit. From this place in us, we can notice how we are seeing and interpreting the world and thus keep tabs on our minds. This is crucial because if you go to sleep and get lost in the reactivity of the mind, you descend quickly into your lower self and suffer accordingly.

Remember, our minds are not always our friends. Every situation we find ourselves in is viewed through the lens of the mind, and this takes into account how we think, how we feel, how we relate, and how we make sense of the world. The mind is often unhappy and looking for trouble, looking to be offended, looking for some injustice or a resentment to be upset about. It tells us stories, and they are quite melodramatic. *He was abusive to me. She shouldn't talk to me that way. How can they justify doing that? What was that idiot thinking? I can't believe he can't see it my way! How can people be so inconsiderate?*

The purpose of the observer is to:

1. **Notice** our thoughts, feelings, images, memories, and body sensations.
2. **Sharpen awareness** of our experience so we have more choices as we attempt to meet needs and wants.
3. **Help us manage** ourselves through natural and healthy self-regulation.

Dionne is a registered nurse with two young children and a husband. She was referred to me by her physician after a suicide attempt. When I asked what brought her to therapy, she replied, "I don't get along with people." Indeed, she fought incessantly with her husband, was alienated from her family-of-origin, and changed jobs about once a year because of conflicts with supervisors. Though she was highly intelligent, Dionne was not very self-smart and, in particular, seemed quite unaware of how she offended everyone. For example, she admitted to being constantly critical of her husband, overly controlling with her kids, and aggressive and confrontational in the workplace.

Progress was slow at first, as Dionne insisted on blaming everyone else for her problems and not taking responsibility for her part. A breakthrough happened when she verbally attacked me for not filling out a leave-of-absence form necessary for her employer. She was quite venomous. When I pointed out I could not fill out a form I'd never been given or even been told about, she realized she had forgotten to give it to me. She apologized, to her credit, and I accepted the apology, but I declined her hug at the end of the session because I felt neither safe nor warm toward her given what had just happened.

At the next session, Dionne asked for help, owning for the first time her pattern of being difficult and hard to get along with. I asked her if she was aware of the voice inside her head, the one that was always chattering. She said that it would never shut up and that it did nothing more than look for something to complain about. I asked her to spend a week watching it, just observing the inner voice, knowing that she was the one who watched, not the inner voice itself. I told her not to feel any pressure to stop the voice, since it is impossible, and to resist the impulse to make immediate changes.

Dionne came to the next session with a dramatic insight; namely, the mental voice was an attempt to defend herself—sort of a the-best-defense-is-a-good-offense strategy. With practice, she got better at observing and realizing there was a difference between the angry emotions she felt and who she actually was. Because she was more aware, she had time to process what was happening to her and then to choose to express herself differently. For instance, instead of yelling, "You never help with the kids!" to her beleaguered husband (who in reality was more attentive to the kids than she), she would step back, reflect, and say something like, "I'm really fried from work today. Would you mind fixing dinner tonight?"

Dionne had become more mindful, in other words, more aware of her experience without judging it. She could still be reactive, a lifelong pattern of behavior, but she could detach from the reactivity. To explain: she might be frustrated with her husband for not doing something, but the observer part of her gave her time to collect herself before attacking him. Instead of lashing out (being lost in the movie in her head), she could observe her frustration as if she had tossed a ball in a stream and watched it float away. She would also say to herself: *Good one, mind…you're telling me Fred is the worst husband ever because he won't mow the lawn tonight.* This new way allowed her to regulate her emotions rather than be ruled by them. Her marriage improved, her parenting improved, and her self-esteem took a quantum leap!

The same approach worked on the job. The observer allowed Dionne to monitor her stress levels and stop herself before acting out from anger toward her patients, fellow staff, the doctors, and the administrators. Interestingly, several other nurses asked her if she was on some new medication, as they had noticed a dramatic difference. In fact, she had gotten off medication, as her symptoms weren't really due to organic imbalances but rather to personality factors and a lack of self-awareness and self-responsibility.

When you identify the observer in you and turn up the knob on self-awareness, you put yourself in a position to make changes you never dreamed possible. Instead of having a thought and just acting on it without consciousness, you can watch it and let it go. You make a conscious decision to take a deep breath and choose a different path than the one that gets you in trouble and prolongs your suffering. Now you watch the movie in your head rather than live it out as if you are your lower self and nothing else. Perhaps the greatest gift of tuning in from the perspective of the observer is that you give yourself a chance to access your higher self—the one that is less reactive and judgmental, more loving and more peaceful. If it worked for Dionne, who changed from a miserable creature of habit to a more enjoyable and happy person; it can work for you too.

29
Are You Grounded?

Energy is the essence of life. Every day you decide how you're going to use it by knowing what you want and what it takes to reach that goal, and by maintaining focus.

—Oprah Winfrey

To be able to function at your highest level and fulfill your potential, it is necessary to be grounded. Being grounded helps you to protect yourself, plan well, achieve goals, and be focused and empowered. Grounding is an important component of effective communication and problem-solving. To be grounded means to be firmly supported by correct posture, proper breathing, a relaxed body, and an alert mind.

Some people use "not being grounded" as a pseudo-coping mechanism. This comes from a childhood survival mechanism of not feeling their feelings or not facing a problem. They have operated this way most of their life and are so comfortable with being flighty or scattered that they don't know that there is any other way. The overuse of alcohol or drugs undermines a sense of being grounded and can contribute to "scatterbrain."

Sally had a girlfriend who had a long history of being flighty and scattered. They left her apartment in California to drive to Mexico. This girlfriend left a pot of boiling water on the stove. After turning around and driving back to the apartment, she realized she'd locked herself out. She broke a window to get in, turned off the stove, and they started out again on the trip. On the way to Ensenada, the girlfriend was speeding and got a ticket. She left the map at home and got lost. By the time they got to Ensenada, they were fighting, frustrated, and hungry. Sally advised her girlfriend to be careful of what she ate at the restaurant they attended.

Her girlfriend did not heed her advice and threw up several times on the way home. While in Ensenada, she left her wallet at one of the stores and after much deliberation decided not to go back and get it. Sally's girl-friend is intelligent, talented, and able. However, this experience left Sally feeling angry that she had not recognized sooner that her friend wasn't grounded and that all this stress and drama were inevitable.

My husband, Bill, describes the following experiences when he is not grounded: a block of ice in his stomach; uncontrolled, free-floating anxiety; and unexplained irritability. These are his personal cues that alert him that he needs to attend to himself. He then meditates, does aerobic exercises, works in the garden, reads spiritual passages, and asks himself, "What is going on?"

We lose our grounding when someone says or does something that triggers our emotional issues. Also, when life gets difficult and connects with our issues. Here are common examples of personal cues that will tell you that you're not grounded:

1. Feeling scattered
2. Feeling flighty
3. Feeling like you are not connected to yourself
4. Feeling like you are not connected to your skin
5. Feeling nausea when you know you are not sick
6. Feeling fear when you know there is nothing to be afraid of
7. Feeling irritable when there is nothing to be irritable about
8. Feeling lightheaded without there being a physical reason
9. Feeling detached, as if you are in a dream
10. Feeling that you are reacting to a situation more than it warrants
11. Feeling like you cannot function and you don't know why
12. Feeling foggy and like you can't get clear
13. Feeling like you are moving through setting cement
14. Feeling like you are not grounded in your body
15. Feeling like you are standing back watching yourself
16. Feeling like you are not fully present
17. Feeling like you are not connected to people around you
18. Feeling like you are not connected to your surroundings

19. Feeling frozen and like you cannot move
20. Not feeling

Get to know your personal cues that tell you when you are not grounded. Also, determine what might trigger this condition. There are several common reasons why you may not be grounded. You might be:

1. Experiencing fear
2. Experiencing anger
3. Experiencing sadness
4. Experiencing depression
5. Experiencing anxiousness
6. Being triggered about something from the past
7. Not wanting to feel feelings
8. Using an old coping skill from the past
9. Avoiding intimacy
10. Avoiding responsibility
11. Experiencing stress overload
12. Feeling emotional overload
13. Feeling ill
14. Experiencing grief or loss
15. Undergoing life transitions
16. Disorganized
17. Disconnected
18. Relying on drugs or alcohol
19. Experiencing shame or humiliation
20. Suffering from post-traumatic stress

Here are several practical ways to get grounded:

1. Exercising
2. Journaling
3. Practicing relaxed breathing
4. Reading inspirational quotations

5. Using self-talk ("I am not grounded. What can I do right now that will ground me? I need to pull myself together now.")

6. Using any religious or spiritual rituals that are grounding (smudging, Qi Gong, meditation, burning candles, and so on)

7. Praying (the Serenity Prayer is excellent for grounding)

8. Using guided imagery that will help you pull yourself together.

9. Checking in with yourself when you get up in the morning and when you go to bed at night, using imagery of being whole

10. Slowing down and being aware of hearing sounds, smelling smells, feeling your body sitting in a chair, and touching items that will ground your body and mind into the present

11. Petting an animal

12. Hugging someone safe

13. Talking to a friend about what is upsetting you

14. Talking to a counselor or a minister

15. Going to a Twelve Step meeting

16. Attending church

17. Gardening

18. Taking a nap

19. Engaging in a favorite hobby

20. Getting in touch with your higher self/spiritual self/wise part, and engaging in dialogue with that part

21. Listening to calming music/playing music

22. Getting and keeping current an organizer/calendar

23. Standing with both feet flat on the floor and touching the palms of your hands to a wall

24. Cleaning/sorting/decluttering

25. Cooking mindfully

26. Holding a favorite rock or token

27. Standing and embracing self with knees slightly bent

28. Walking barefoot while touching the earth

29. Standing like a tree with your arms extended (knees slightly flexed)

30. Pretending you are an animal (you are), and crawling on the ground

Are You Grounded?
Worksheet

Cues	Triggers	Getting Grounded
EX: Nauseated	Anxious about family visiting	Meditating, self-talk, taking breaks, relaxed breathing

1. _____ _____ _____
   _____ _____ _____

2. _____ _____ _____
   _____ _____ _____

3. _____ _____ _____
   _____ _____ _____

4. _____ _____ _____
   _____ _____ _____

5. _____ _____ _____
   _____ _____ _____

6. _____ _____ _____
   _____ _____ _____

7. _____ _____ _____
   _____ _____ _____

8. _____ _____ _____
   _____ _____ _____

30
Numbing Out

That's the great paradox of living on this earth, that in the midst of great pain you can have great joy as well. If we didn't have those things we'd just be numb.

—Kathy Mattea

I learned to be with myself rather than avoid myself with limiting habits; I started to be aware of my feelings more, rather than numb them.

—Judith Wright

We usually think of being numbed out as a negative thing, but it is also a survival skill that allows us to cope while experiencing a trauma or at a time when we are enduring abusive behavior. When we think of *numb* as an adjective, it means we are unable to think or feel or sense in a normal way, which is adaptive if being fully present to the painful event would be overwhelming.

Consider a young girl who is being touched inappropriately by a favorite uncle. Numbing out allows her to experience her fear, rage, shame, confusion, and sense of betrayal less intensely. Perhaps without numbing, she would feel overwhelmed and end up even more injured. As a verb, *to numb* refers to how we make ourselves less responsive to a painful experience. The same girl, assuming she showed good self-awareness, might later report on her experience by saying, "Numbing out deadened the pain in my heart."

Numbing out often occurs in situations where, as children, we lacked the safety, security, and support needed to cope with painful or traumatic circumstances. Those circumstances could be physical (being struck by an angry parent), emotional (feeling emotionally abandoned by a self-absorbed caretaker who ignores your sad expression), sexual (being fondled by a grown-up you know and trust), or spiritual (being told you will "burn in hell" because you were caught in a lie). All of these examples would make it more likely that a vulnerable child would numb out emotionally, especially if there was no one to go to for validation and support. We can see how this can sometimes be a healthy defense. The problem is that numbing out can become chronic, a part of a person's character.

When we numb out as grown-ups in situations that don't call for that level of defense, then the numbing is chronic and not considered healthy. It has become anachronistic (from Greek "ana," or backward, and "khronos," time). If we make a habit of numbing out, it is anachronistic; that is, it's the wrong time to do it. It made sense when we were a vulnerable child; it is not necessary as a more resourceful adult. Defenseless children become more resourceful adults but often continue to think of themselves as if they were just as vulnerable as in childhood.

Hannah is a client in her late forties who survived a mother who would hit her with a tennis racquet and for no good reason. As a child, Hannah became almost impervious to pain by numbing herself out via dissociation. It was as if she said to her sadistic mother, "Go ahead and hit me; it doesn't hurt because I'm not really in my body." This worked in a way, in that Hannah minimized the enormity of the abuse she endured and also because the mother stopped hitting the girl because it didn't seem to bother her. Now Hannah has a boyfriend, but she is so emotionally numb that nothing seems to affect her at all. If he treats her wonderfully, it seemingly has no impact on her. This understandably frustrates him. If he threatens to end the relationship because she won't invest emotionally, she acts like she doesn't care. Moreover, Hannah restricts herself to 1500 calories a day and works out obsessively. To make matters worse, she drinks a bit too much, consuming three or four glasses of red wine every evening. Consider the following list of symptoms for being numbed out and how many describe Hannah:

1. **"Under the influence"** of any chemical, legal or otherwise, on a regular basis

2. **Speeded up**—seeking an adrenaline rush can be as addictive and numbing as any chemical; this could be through "workaholism," video gaming, risky behaviors, frantic socialization, or manic partying

3. **Eating issues or food addictions** can be an extremely effective numbing device over years

4. **Creating chaos and crisis**—ongoing lawsuits, continuing to be upset with what others say or do, upsetting others, having to clean up messes, and so on

5. **Being accident prone**—continuous injuries, hospitalizations, and so on

6. **Ongoing physical issues** with or without medical basis

7. **Gambling addiction** of any kind

8. **Sex addictions**—abuse or excessive use of computer porn, porn books, sex magazines, compulsive masturbation, and so on

9. **Not being grounded**—flighty, drifty, or scattered

10. **Being disconnected**—failure to make real connections with friends, family, and coworkers; such persons are told they are "space cases," "not fully present," "on another planet," "in the ozone layer," and so on

11. **Feeling like you are above looking down at yourself**—during stressful situations or ones where a person is triggered, he or she may numb to the point of detaching from his or her body

12. **Obsessing** about other people's issues or about your own issues— this can be a way of going into your head and away from the felt experience of the body

13. **Overrescuing** others—this can be a numbing strategy if it serves to distract you from your own feelings

14. **Compulsive buying**—when triggered, buying things instead of dealing with what is bothering you, thus avoiding difficult or painful feelings

15. **Ongoing obsessive relationships** in which you are continuously falling in love with someone instead of facing your issues

When you recognize that you are numbing out, you can use Chapter 24 entitled "Checking in with Yourself" and the worksheet: "Helpful Questions to Ask When Triggered." With Hannah, we focused on getting her to lean into any "ouch" experiences, whether they were old or new. I actually became annoying to her by repeatedly asking questions such as, "How did that register in your body?" "What emotions came up when he said that to you?" "What's going on in your body right now?" "Could you lean into your anger and see how it feels?" "I notice your jaw is clenched. Could you clench it even tighter and tell me what comes up for you?"

In time, Hannah learned to experience herself as a feeling woman, rather than automatically numbing out in the service of protecting her vulnerable self. Her relationship with her boyfriend failed, but she is more alive now and will have many more chances to connect and find a satisfying relationship.

For Presence

Awaken to the mystery of being here
And enter the quiet immensity of your own presence.

Have joy and peace in the temple of your senses.

Receive encouragement when new frontiers beckon.

Respond to the call of your gift and the courage to
Follow its path.

Let the flame of anger free you of all falsity.

May warmth of heart keep your presence aflame.

May anxiety never linger about you.

May your outer dignity mirror an inner dignity of
Soul.

Take time to celebrate the quiet miracles that seek
No attention.

Be consoled in the secret symmetry of your soul.

May you experience each day as a sacred gift woven
Around the heart of wonder.

—John O'Donohue

31
Selfish, Selfless, and Self-Caring

Selfishness is not living as one wishes to live, it is asking others to live as one wishes to live.

—Oscar Wilde

When we finally learn that self-care begins and ends with ourselves, we no longer demand sustenance and happiness from others.

—Jennifer Louden

Mona complains that Jim, her husband of twenty-five years, is a "selfish pig." When asked to make her case, she tells me, "The other night, I hurt my shoulder moving a sofa, and when we went to bed, I asked him to massage it. He said, 'Me first,' so I gave him a massage, and he fell asleep. In the morning, when I complained that I never got my massage, he told me to 'lighten up.'" She went on to give many more examples, and I had to believe Jim was, in fact, selfish with an exclamation point! The real question became, was it possible for Mona to get him to change his ways, given that he'd been a selfish man throughout their marriage?

People like Jim almost always grow up in homes that lacked emotional support and love. Their needs are rarely met as children, and they are typically disappointed or frustrated if they try to get their needs met. They grow up angry, lacking empathy, and expecting the world to give them what they did not get. Selfishness becomes a strategy to get what they need. An attitude of entitlement develops, as if the world should give them everything.

A less frequent dynamic is that some selfish people were overindulged and came to believe the world revolved around their needs. Either way, they become focused on meeting their own needs at the expense of others and rarely consider others' feelings. They make demands and expect them to be fulfilled. Because they are weak, they try to control others in order to feel strong. Because they are insecure, they are willing to step on others if it will make them feel more secure. Selfishness can lead to material success but never to fulfillment in the areas of intimacy.

Selfish people unconsciously seek and find mates who are selfless, and such was the case with Mona. These people, often the women, learned they must give up who they really are in order to feel loved or accepted. They then focus on the needs and wants of others, as if an unconscious deal has been struck: "I will give up asserting who I am and what I want if you promise to never leave me." Being selfless means they stop asserting a self, namely expressing their wants, needs, values, opinions, and voice. They don't define themselves for fear of being abandoned; hence, they can't set limits or express true feelings. In Mona's marriage, her selflessness enabled Jim to be abusive, controlling, and manipulative. That's not to say it is Mona's fault, but she played a big part in the problem.

Our goal was to get Mona to be more self-caring by risking a commitment to her own personal mental health. This meant defining her self by strongly asserting what she needed from Jim and also what she would and wouldn't tolerate from him. Obviously, we had to prepare her for the possibility that Jim would not change and that she might have to face the world on her own.

Self-care is not the same as being selfish because it considers the other person. Some people learn self-care by growing up in a family that meets most of their needs and teaches respectful communication. Mona didn't get this in her family-of-origin, so she had to learn through education and practice.

A key moment occurred when she asked Jim to take a day off work to take her to the doctor's office for a minor surgical procedure, where she felt insecure about driving herself home. When he balked, she made it known she would be very disappointed if he refused. He still refused, so Mona, per our session discussions, gave him an ultimatum: either he would take her and start considering what she needed from him or she would move out. He laughed. She moved out and discovered that life without Jim wasn't as lonely and frightening as she had thought. Mona has filed for divorce and is continuing to assert herself. She is not divorcing to punish Jim but to take care of herself. She realized Jim was not THE problem, the problem was her fear of being alone.

In summary, it is crucial that you learn to distinguish between selfish, selfless, and self-caring. Like Mona, take note of your old patterns of relating to yourself and others and commit to healthy self-care. If you notice you are not taking care of yourself or failing to consider the needs of others, make a conscious choice to change. Use others as a sounding board and get feedback on how you are seen: selfish, selfless, or self-caring. Look for symptoms of something that seems off in your life. Examples would be physical ailments, depression, anxiety, loneliness, addiction issues, or self-destructive behavior. These are cues to ramp up your self-care program and commit to personal health maintenance.

It is also helpful to surround yourself with examples of people you admire and respect and observe their behavior as a benchmark of healthy self-care. If you are involved with a Jim or someone else whose selfishness is costing you your health or happiness, confront the person and give him or her the opportunity to make changes. If the person makes changes, you've improved your life and his or hers. If the person fails to take the opportunity, you may face some difficult choices about staying in the relationship. Remember that selfishness is weakness, selflessness is a prescription for depression, and healthy self-care is necessary for a life of fulfillment. There's a reason the airline companies instruct you to put your own oxygen mask on first!

32
Green Is Good
(Turning Jealousy into a Positive)

Jealousy, that dragon which slays love under the pretence of keeping it alive.
—Havelock Ellis

Don't waste your dissatisfaction, use it as fuel.

—Thom Rutledge

Do you try to control the actions of your partner for fear he or she might find someone else? Do you worry whether you're sufficiently attractive or successful to hold on to your partner? Do you compare yourself to others of the same sex and fear you could lose your partner to a rival? Is your sense of worth so low you feel you could easily be replaced in your relationship? If you notice your significant other looking at persons of the opposite sex, do you get a sick, vulnerable feeling? If you answered "yes" to any of these questions, you're struggling with the experience of jealousy.

Jealousy comes from feeling unworthy of respect and undeserving of love. These aspects of low self-esteem lead to a "jealousy triangle," composed of the jealous person, a beloved partner, and a rival. Three people are involved, whereas in envy, it's usually two. Jealousy typically involves the desire to hold on to what you already possess, whereas envy implies wanting something you covet but don't have. For example, a wife is jealous of her husband's attention to the next-door neighbor and becomes watchful or possessive for fear of losing him. She is envious of the woman's brand-new Mercedes. Her jealousy and envy make her unhappy and angry and can easily bring about the demise of an otherwise good relationship.

Most jealous persons believe it's their disposition or nature and that once afflicted, they are doomed to act out jealously for life. Not true, and although jealousy looks entirely negative and destructive, recall that there are no gratuitous emotions. All have a purpose in guiding our social interactions and allowing us to respond appropriately to our circumstances. Jealousy is no exception and, with awareness, can be used in a productive and adaptive way.

An example will show us how. Muriel has been with her boyfriend, Matt, for over two years. The relationship goes well enough, but Muriel feels threatened by Matt's friendliness with other women at the gym where they work out. She is jealous of the time and attention Matt gives anyone other than her. Muriel's choice is to allow her jealousy to consume her and spoil the relationship or to use the feeling as a cue to resolve her insecurities. Here are some steps for Muriel to turn her jealousy into a positive for emotional growth:

1. **Be aware of jealousy and treat it like a cue.** Muriel recognizes her jealousy is an indication of low self-esteem stemming from unmet needs in her family-of-origin.

2. **Identify what wants and needs are not being met.** Muriel wants more of Matt but simultaneously realizes he is doing nothing wrong in being friendly. She owns her problem, telling Matt she is going to work on it.

3. **Set up a plan to deal with her underlying issues.** Muriel decides to watch her self-talk with the goal of improving feelings of worth. Whenever she is self-critical, she asks, "What is the evidence for that?" She disputes negative self-statements on a consistent basis and affirms her worth. She finds a good book on improving self-esteem and commits to reading it. She sets a realistic time frame for improvement and agrees to enter counseling if she can't do it on her own.

4. **Think of jealousy as an intrapsychic rather than interpersonal problem.** In other words, it is between Muriel and her mind (which generates automatic negative thoughts), rather than between Muriel and Matt. This reframe will help you own the problem and focus on changing your behavior and thoughts rather than trying to control someone else's.

5. **Resist the urge to control the object of your jealousy.** When Muriel observed Matt being friendly with other women, part of her wanted to stop him so she wouldn't have to feel afraid of being displaced. In time, she came to realize the real solution was to watch jealousy unfold, relax her heart, and let go. In this way she learned to surrender to the flow of life (since trying to control it only increased her suffering!).

Jealousy is a common affliction and can often be handled with self-awareness and the following worksheet, but in some people, the feeling becomes so corrosive it can wreck their relationships and lives. It would be misleading for me to suggest you can heal a serious jealousy problem after reading this brief chapter.

I do, however, believe you can identify your problem here and seek out the counseling help you will need to work on the deep-seated inferiority complex that underlies pathological jealousy. This complex, which leaves you feeling inadequate, insecure, and threatened, is not your fault. It is a leftover from unmet childhood needs that can be worked through in a safe and corrective relationship with a good therapist. If you had a toothache, you'd go to the dentist. Smart people get help.

Green Is Good
(Turning Jealousy into a Positive)
Worksheet

1. Cue (Physical or Emotional)_____

_____

_____

2. Unmet Need/Want_____

_____

_____

3. List of Negative Consequences (If I Continue to Act Out My Jealousy)

_____

_____

_____

_____

_____

_____

4. Make a Plan (Include List of What Needs to Be Accomplished and Time Frame)

What Needs to Be Accomplished   **Time Frame**

_____   _____

_____   _____

_____   _____

_____   _____

_____   _____

33
Fear Is No Burden

You gain strength, courage and confidence by every experience in which you really stop to look fear in the face. You must do the thing you think you cannot do.

—Eleanor Roosevelt

If fear is cultivated it will become stronger, if faith is cultivated it will achieve mastery. It seems to be a law of nature, inflexible and inexorable, that those who will not risk cannot win.

—John Paul Jones

Eleanor Roosevelt, by all accounts a painfully shy and awkward child, conquered fear and insecurity to become the much-respected and admired first lady to President Franklin D. Roosevelt. Eleanor's early life was not one that fostered a sense of security and self-confidence. Her mother died when she was eight, and her alcoholic father died before she turned ten. As a teen, she was sent off to be formally educated at an English finishing school, where she knew no one. She returned to America and served as a social worker in the dangerous east side slums of New York.

When she was thirty-four, with five children ranging in age from five to fifteen, her husband, Franklin, suffered a paralytic illness. In part due to his restricted mobility, Eleanor redefined the role of first lady. She overcame her shyness to make numerous public appearances on her husband's behalf, held pressure-packed press conferences, lectured around the world, did radio broadcasts heard by millions, and wrote a daily syndicated newspaper column. She took on controversial topics, such as civil rights for African Americans long before the civil rights movement, and championed human rights. Eleanor Roosevelt's legacy is not only for her contributions as first lady in an era when few women pursued careers but also for her refusal to give in to fear.

Fear can be a gift, not a burden to bear, because it is a God-given warning signal that trumpets real or perceived danger. When we receive subtle or not-so-subtle intuitions that something or someone is amiss, we must honor them. Then again, sometimes we experience fear, and there appears to be no good reason. "I'm afraid to ride the roller coaster at the amusement park or afraid to speak up and ask the professor a question in statistics class." Regardless of the "reasonableness" of such fears, they do not come out of nowhere and are wired into us for a reason, so take them seriously by asking a series of questions:

- **What am I afraid of?** A new hire at a marketing agency is asked to make a presentation to the entire staff on guerilla marketing using cutting-edge mobile digital technologies. Just out of college, she is terrified *(fear of embarrassment)*. A recently divorced woman meets a man online, and they meet for coffee. When it's time to leave, he tells her he feels "destined" to spend his life with her. Her stomach does flip-flops *(fear of being stalked by a creep)*. A fifty-year-old woman with back problems has trouble lifting a heavy box from her shopping cart to the trunk of her car. A charming young man offers to help, but they are alone in a poorly lit parking garage, and she has an uneasy feeling about him *(fear of physical attack)*. A young housewife with a toddler is afraid to venture out of her home to shop for groceries *(fear of having a panic attack in public)*. Knowing what it is you are afraid of and what would happen if your worst fear materialized will inform subsequent decision-making.

- **Should I give in to the fear?** In each of the above scenarios, our heroine must assess her situation and make a choice based on what is most likely generating her fear *(suggested in parenthesis above)*. Collecting more information would be useful but isn't always feasible. The woman asked to make a presentation can prepare her speech and get support, but the woman in the deserted parking lot must make a snap decision. We are wise to consider what percentage of the time our fears would realistically take place. For instance, many people are afraid of flying but do so anyway because they know the risk of a plane crash is actually quite low.

- **If the fear is real, what can I do about it?** Hopefully you have prepared for possibly dangerous events. If you are hiking in the mountains and come upon a big momma black bear with her cub, you would be well advised to already know you must make yourself look big, generate noise, and get out your bear-repellent spray. For that matter, our heroine in the parking garage, we hope, has pepper spray in her purse and knows how to use it if the Good Samaritan turns out to be a rotten egg with a bad agenda.

- **If it is real but there is nothing I can do about it, then let it go and focus on what I can do.** I recall reading in an autobiography how a violent and predatory man cornered a woman in a public restroom. As he came at her, she said, "In the name of God, please don't hurt me." He stopped in his tracks and then left. I am currently treating a woman in her early seventies who suffers a driving phobia. Her fear of other drivers is real, and she can't make others drive more sensibly, but she is taking a driver's education course specifically designed for elders to improve her own skills and self-confidence.

- **Have a backup plan.** If what you have prepared for doesn't seem to be working, what else can you do? The woman in the coffee shop who fears her online "date" is a stalker can ask a manager to escort her to her car. The woman in the parking garage might have a panic button on her automobile's keyless entry system, or she might have taken a self-defense class and knows to yell for help and to resist any attempt to isolate her. The young mother with agoraphobia (*the fear of developing panic-like or embarrassing symptoms in public*) could seek counseling help to cope with this very treatable condition.

Now that we've identified some questions, we can better assess and respond to whatever situation is generating fear. In many instances, there is even time to put pencil to paper and think it out. When my college-age daughter went to Costa Rica to do community service work in a rain forest reserve, she understandably had fears about going away for the first time without her parents. She used this fear list to cope with her anxiety and to prepare effectively for the trip. She used the list like this:

Fear List	Is it Real?	Can I do Anything About it?	To Do List	Backup Plan(s)
1. Illness	Yes	Yes	Get Inoculations/Take Medicine	Know Where Local Hospital is
2. Insect Bites	Yes	Yes	Repellant/Bite Kit/Sleeping Net	Locate Doctor
3. Hurricane	Yes	Yes	Check Weather Reports	Find Shelter
4. Kidnappers	Yes	Yes	File a Trip Report	Carry a Cell Phone
5. Language Barrier	Yes	Yes	Study Spanish/Take a List of Basic Survival Words	English/Spanish Dictionary or App on Phone
6. Market Shopping	No	Yes	Dispute Negative Self-Talk	Seek Professional Help

Fear Is No Burden Worksheet

Fear List	Is It Real? Yes/No	Can I Do Anything About It?	To Do List	Backup Plan
1.				
2.				
3.				
4.				
5.				
6.				
7.				
8.				
9.				
10.				

Self-Talk Exercise

1. Ask: "What is the worst thing that could happen? Can I survive it? I won't like it, but I can survive it."

_____

_____

_____

_____

2. Ask yourself again: "What is the next worse fear? Can I survive that?" And so forth.

_____

_____

_____

_____

3. Remember to get reality checks (is it real or not?) on the information you've collected.

_____

_____

_____

_____

4. Self-talk on this issue as many times as necessary and prepare accordingly (see chapter 20, "Self-Talk").

"I will honor my intuitions and consider fear a gift and a guide."
"I will only give in to fear when it tells me I'm in real danger."
"I will summon the most resourceful parts of myself to deal with fear."
"I can survive this if I live in reality and practice reality-based thoughts."
"I will be OK if I make the right choices."

"I will prepare for every possibility."

"If I don't know what the reality of the situation is, I will ask someone who does know or collect information on my own." (Write down what the person said, and practice "reality-based self-talk.")

_____

_____

_____

_____

_____

34
Making Mistakes Skillfully

A mistake is simply a failure to approach a problem correctly the first time.
—Igor Stravinsky

We should not feel embarrassed by our difficulties,
Only by our failure to grow anything beautiful from them.
—Alain de Botton

Being human, we all make mistakes, which makes perfectionism a curse. Simply stated, you will always make mistakes and can never achieve the ideal of perfection. The issue is therefore not to eliminate mistakes but to greet them with compassion and wisdom. As I compose the words on this page, I make typing errors. Do I beat myself up for not being a better typist or backspace and correct the error without judgment? I have a choice. I can judge my mistakes and suffer, or accept them with a chuckle and be at peace. Making mistakes skillfully means responding to them without aversion, judgment, or self-condemnation. It means taking responsibility without becoming self-blaming.

Laura grew up with a critical father who expected perfection. "It wasn't just getting straight A's and becoming valedictorian," she told me. "The nap had to be going in the same direction if I vacuumed the carpet." Counseling focused on disputing the family "no mistakes" rule and forgiving herself on those occasions when she really did goof up. A breakthrough came when Laura dropped two envelopes into a mailbox only to realize she'd forgotten to put stamps on them. "At first, I said to myself, 'You stupid, stupid…' and then I caught myself. It was like my father was with me, berating me, and I laughed and told him, 'It's no big deal! They'll return the letters, and I'll stamp them and mail them again.'" In essence, Laura had replaced the critical father voice with a more allowing and forgiving grown-up voice—her voice. This is the work.

Here are some steps to take to make mistakes skillfully:

1. **Admit to yourself that you made a mistake.** Once you accept the notion that it's OK to be fallible, it's not such a big deal to acknowledge your blunders. This is especially important when you are the only person involved. Say "yes" to your mistakes, and feel the sense of peace. This is the path of surrendering.

2. **Take responsibility by acknowledging your mistake** to those affected, assuming it does not result in injury to you. For example, you wouldn't tell your insanely jealous boyfriend you had too much to drink at a New Year's Eve party and passionately kissed his best friend. Taking responsibility would be to disclose your mistake to a trusted friend or counselor (who, I hope, will help you get out of this toxic relationship). If your mistake impacts others, take responsibility by acknowledging it to them. "I'm sorry; I spaced out and painted your kitchen the wrong color. I'll repaint it tomorrow. The good news is it will have an extra coat!" If you can't tell anyone, write a letter of apology you have no intention of sending.

3. **Accept a moment of shame** if that's what you honestly feel. Shame is a useful feeling in that it informs you that you did something you ought not to have done, something that violated your own code of conduct (like shoplifting, talking behind a friend's back, driving double the speed limit, or having an affair). Calling yourself names will only lower your self-esteem and make change more difficult.

4. **Forgive yourself.** Be gentle. You are fallible, imperfect. Let yourself off the hook, and by all means, watch your self-talk. Say only what you would to someone you love dearly, such as your best friend or child. Here are some helpful affirmations: "I'm only human, and

humans make mistakes." "It's OK to make the same mistake more than once." "I regret making this mistake, and I'm going to learn how to do it differently the next time." "Making mistakes is the way I learn." "If God can forgive me, I ought to be able to forgive myself." Say these affirmations often, and wire them into your brain. This is the path of self-acceptance.

5. **Learn from your mistakes.** Be curious about what caused them. Mistakes are an opportunity for learning, whether you installed your new sparkplugs improperly or placed an extra zero on your tax return. Were you careless, unprepared, or just lacking in the necessary skills? Were you in too big a hurry? Did you take on a task without adequate preparation? Maybe you could read a manual or get advice from an expert, but don't beat up on yourself for being human. Ask yourself what circumstances triggered the behavior? Did an earlier mistake result in a second, more serious one? A friend had too many glasses of wine at a fundraiser (a lapse in judgment), drove home intoxicated, and rear-ended another motorist (committing a crime and injuring an elderly couple). Mistakes are repeated until learned, so let's hope my friend learned her lesson.

6. **Find a solution for the mistake, and commit to change.** Let's say you have a pattern of choosing men who control you with displays of anger and intimidation. One solution might be to write out a list of negative consequences (I could get physically hurt. I'm afraid to express my opinions. My friends have lost respect for me. I've lost respect for myself...). Then, anytime you're tempted to continue a relationship with such a man, take out your list and remind yourself why you need to make a healthier choice. Stand up to the unhealthy choice. Remember the AA aphorism: "Insanity is continuing to repeat the same behavior while expecting a different outcome."

Shaming yourself or others will not lead to learning and personal growth. Make friends with your mistakes. Have a little chuckle when you spill the milk, lose your car keys, or say something embarrassing in front of the boss. Accept your fallible nature without judgment, and use it to learn something new. Making mistakes skillfully means responding mindfully, with compassion and wisdom. We will continue to make mistakes until the day we die so acceptance is the key to higher consciousness and inner peace.

The Navajo have a wonderful tradition of sewing an intentional error into their magnificent woven rugs. They do so because they do not consider perfection to be the absence of imperfection but the acceptance of it. Greet your mistakes with an attitude of acceptance, and watch yourself rise above the shame that comes with useless self-criticism. To do otherwise will doom you to low self-esteem and a lifetime of needless suffering.

Making Mistakes Skillfully Worksheet

1. Admit to yourself that you made a mistake. "My mistake was…"

_____

_____

_____

_____

2. Take responsibility by acknowledging your mistake to those affected, assuming it does not result in injury to you or others.

_____

_____

_____

_____

3. Accept a moment of shame if that's what you honestly feel.

_____

_____

_____

_____

4. Forgive yourself.

_____

_____

_____

_____

5. Learn from your mistakes. "Here are my lessons…"

_____

_____

_____

_____

6. Find a solution for the mistake, and commit to change.

_____

_____

_____

_____

Reminder: focus on learning and the solution.

35
Mom's Comfort List
(When Away from Home)

When you're down and troubled
And you need a helping hand
And nothing, whoa nothing is going right.
Close your eyes and think of me
And soon I will be there
To brighten up…even your darkest nights.

—James Taylor

Oh the comfort, the inexpressible comfort of feeling safe with a person, having neither to weigh thoughts nor measure words, but pouring them all right out, just as they are.

—Dinah Maria Mulock

Being homesick isn't like having a head cold or the stomach flu; it's usually worse, because there's no guarantee it will be gone or better in a week. And homesickness doesn't just happen to kids at summer camp and high school grads beginning life at university. Even grown-ups will feel homesick at some time in their lives and will yearn for what feels safe and secure, while they long for the comforts of home and routine.

Animals also feel homesick from time to time. I travel a fair amount, and if I'm gone for an extended period of time, Jack, one my three Brussels Griffon therapy dogs, will mope and refuse to eat. It's usually the separation from those to whom we are attached that causes this reaction, and none of us are immune. But homesickness can also be triggered by the loss of what is familiar—our own bed, the swingset in our backyard, or our scratched and cluttered desk in the workplace.

Feeling homesick can be even more painful if we already have a lot on our plate. The child who is at camp because he has a serious illness and the adult who is out of town on business while his wife is about to deliver a baby are both vulnerable to feeling anxious and sad. Now for the good news—you can cope effectively with homesickness by using the following ten ideas:

1. **Practice.** Before attending summer Bible camp or taking an extended business trip, take a trial run by spending a night or two at your best friend's house or an out-of-town hotel.

2. **Bring along a transitional object.** Take along your most comfortable pajamas or travel with your favorite stuffed animal (my editor, Stan, travels with a small, green stuffed dinosaur named Vanilla). Pack a family photo that will remind you that you are loved.

3. **Stay in touch.** Phone home, call a friend, or e-mail or text-message a supportive person. Mom's voice and reassuring tone may comfort you, but don't overdo it or your anxiety and sadness won't work themselves through.

4. **Journal.** There is a wonderful saying, "I put my feelings down on paper." Do it to get in touch with what or whom you're homesick for and act accordingly, e.g., if it's your dog Scruffy you miss so much, have Mom mail or e-mail you a photo or lock of hair.

5. **Keep busy.** Get involved and stay active. Sign up for volleyball, or read a good book. If you're not doing anything fun or exciting, you have more time to dwell on the object of your longing.

6. **Share.** Tell someone what you're experiencing. Let the camp counselor know you're homesick or self-disclose to a business

partner how much you miss your wife and kids. This connection alone will reduce the feelings of loneliness.

7. **Visit your "wise part."** Listen to the voice that emanates from a wise place within. Honor your intuitions. Ask yourself what Mom, Dad, or a respected mentor would advise you to say or do to cope more effectively.

8. **Watch your self-talk.** You will do better if you pay attention to the thoughts your mind is producing. Is your mind telling you, "I can't stand this another minute!" or "I can get through this; these feelings won't last forever!" Whichever you believe, you'll be right.

9. **Soothe yourself.** Comfort your mind, body, and spirit by taking time to sit quietly, take a nap, meditate, pray, listen to soft music, breathe deeply, burn a lavender candle, or get a hug or a massage.

10. **Still homesick?** If suggestions 1 through 9 don't do the trick (and they almost always will), consult a professional counselor or psychologist. This is especially important if you can't sleep or eat or are developing physical symptoms, such as stomachaches or headaches.

Remember, almost everyone, child and adult, deals with homesickness at one time or another. It is a normal feeling and even has a good side because it means you have people in your life who love and care for you and familiar surroundings you associate with safety and security. By the way, this list of suggestions not only works when you're feeling homesick but also when you're scared, sad, lonely, tired, or ill. Try them, and prepare for a pleasant surprise!

36
A More Satisfying Life

Success is not the key to happiness. Happiness is the key to success. If you love what you are doing, you will be successful.

—Albert Schweitzer

In spiritual terms, life is not problematic; only our attitudes toward it are.

—Anonymous

Kellie, middle-aged and divorced for nearly ten years, felt sad and lonely until she met Louis, a firefighter ten years her junior. Louis, full of life and even more full of himself, had a way of making her feel young and attractive. He took her for a hot-air-balloon ride on their second date and made passionate love to her while camping in the Cascade Mountains. When things were right between them, Kellie felt on top of the world and immensely satisfied with her life situation. When Louis began to ignore her and express interest in younger women, she slid into a deep depression.

In our first session, we realized Louis's interest or lack of it had become the absolute barometer for Kellie's happiness. With him, she felt whole, never happier. Without him, she felt incomplete, miserable, and unlovable.

Over the next six sessions, we came up with some practical suggestions to help Kellie work her way back to feeling like a whole person. Our goal was to lift her level of happiness so she could lead a more satisfying life, whether or not it involved Louis. Here are those suggestions:

1. **Follow your bliss.** Sage advice from the late mythologist Joseph Campbell. Identify what it is that makes life worth living, and pursue

your dreams. Let nothing get in the way of doing whatever gives meaning to your life, whether it's inventing a better mousetrap, playing chess with friends, doing needlepoint, volunteering for your favorite nonprofit, or overindulging your grandchildren.

2. **Honor your gifts.** You create happiness when you do the things you're good at and gain a feeling of competence and fulfillment. Kellie resumed a longtime interest in photography and put on an exhibition at a nearby library. Instead of dwelling on her conflicted relationship with Louis, she invested her time doing something she loved.

3. **Cultivate meaningful relationships.** You create happiness when you connect with others and enjoy the positive feelings that come from doing something meaningful. Kellie volunteered to teach a photography class to preteens at a community center. She also joined the Mountaineers and went for hikes on weekends with like-minded persons in her age group.

4. **Count your blessings.** Wake up to gratitude. Keep a gratitude journal in which you write down two to three positive experiences a day. Vary your entries to keep them fresh. Use ideas like how beautiful the flowers are, how much you love your children or life partner, what fun it was to play with the puppies, or what a fabulous bowl of soup you had for lunch. This helped Kellie notice and focus on the positives in her life, rather than pining away for Louis.

5. **Celebrate your sense of humor.** Develop the ability to find something to laugh at even in times of trouble, as well as the knack for helping others do the same. Go see a funny movie, watch your favorite sitcom, or read a humorous book. Stand in front of a mirror and speak with a bad French accent. Kellie organized a group of friends who went to see a famous comic perform at a downtown theater.

6. **Savor your best moments.** Relish the times in your life that are truly sweet and satisfying. For example, take time to fully appreciate being with a loved one, phone a friend to share your enjoyment of a gorgeous sunset, or journal about a sensual or sexual experience. Replay these moments often, using all your senses.

7. **Cultivate a love of learning.** Honor your inquisitive side by making a list of things you want to do, and then carry them out. Go back to school, learn a foreign language, take bridge lessons, or teach yourself how to build that backyard deck you've coveted. Kellie had always wanted to learn how to scuba dive. She took a class and parlayed it into a trip to Maui.

8. **Explore your creativity.** Discover your flair for creating something from nothing, for producing something surprising or unusual. Don't be afraid to try something new. Learn to play a musical instrument, take a dance class, join a writing group, or hire an instructor to teach you to paint. Do it with a playful spirit, and don't judge your work.

9. **Develop your philosophical or spiritual side.** This development can be very supportive and helpful when you hit upon bad times or losses. Go on your own personal search or journey by reading books, talking to people, traveling and visiting monasteries, churches or temples, or explore your own space by meditating or doing Yoga in your own backyard. Explore questions that you've had in your life and make your heart open to receive answers. This may very well bring you joy. If you have trouble finding answers, keep your heart open for them to come to you. Allow yourself to feel contentment along the way. Practice living in the present.

You don't really find happiness; you create a way of life that makes you happy. Underline you, because if you think someone else can make you happy, you're mistaken. You can actually make a commitment to being happy and to bring that about practice compassion for yourself and others, cultivate inner peace, release tension and negativity, and keep an open heart.

Kellie had to learn these lessons the hard way, as Louis eventually dropped her so he could play the field. Her depression lifted as she put into practice the suggestions listed here and decided to be happy. Her life became satisfying as she engaged in activities meaningful to her and became the person she was meant to be. In a sense, Kelly developed an inner sanctuary that allowed her to be less dependent on others in order to create her own happiness.

37
Developing Resilience

Possessing a resilient mindset does not imply that one is free from stress, pressure, or conflict, but rather that one can successfully cope with problems as they arise.

—Robert Brooks and Sam Goldstein

One of the hallmarks of good mental health is resilience, which is defined as the ability to bounce back to an effective state of functioning after experiencing hardship. A resilient person typically recovers quickly from difficulty, whether it involves a stressful event, an overwhelming problem, a significant loss, a traumatic experience, or a demanding life transition.

Resilience is often spoken of as if it is a trait that some people have and others don't, but it is really more of a process or a series of steps when faced with adversity. This means we can cultivate or upgrade our resilience by paying attention to the following factors:

1. **Practicing good self-care.** Resilience is promoted when we eat healthy food, practice smart sleep hygiene, exercise regularly, use moderation in alcohol, avoid drugs, and get medical attention when necessary.

2. **Using effective coping skills.** Making a conscious decision to cope effectively with adversity will enhance resilience. Let's say you lose your job unexpectedly and feel devastated. You may be tempted to drink or engage in other avoidance strategies, but you summon the grown-up part of you and network, get out job applications, and

rely on your support system to get you through. Find joy in each day.

3. **Embracing a belief system.** Having a religious, spiritual, or philosophical belief system that can support you through tough times develops resilience. Resilient people pray, use rituals, burn candles and incense, and commune with nature when they need help to cope.

4. **Building and maintaining a support system.** Being connected with family and friends who care fosters resilience. Life is simply too hard to go it alone; we need others to help us through adversity.

5. **Opening up and sharing.** You can build up resilience by self-disclosing your stress, trauma, and life tragedy to another person, as long as the person you choose is caring, supportive, and nonjudgmental. Telling your story can open your heart.

6. **Asking for help.** Those of us who were either frustrated or disappointed when we needed help as children grow up thinking we have to "lick our own wounds." This is a mistake that undermines our resilience. Take the risk of asking family, friends, and church or community agencies for support when you need to spring back from a difficulty.

7. **Accepting life on its own terms.** Accepting circumstances rather than fighting them promotes resilience. For instance, "I don't like it that my sister is addicted to alcohol and Valium, but this is the way she is," demonstrates acceptance as opposed to, "I hate my sister's addictions; she should get her act together and stop ruining the family." Try the Serenity Prayer: "God grant me the serenity to accept the things I cannot change, courage to change the things I can, and wisdom to know the difference."

8. **Having the ability to let go**. Resilience is fostered by letting go, and one of the best ways is to turn over to your Higher Power that which seems too much to bear. Suppose someone you love is dying and you seemingly can't cope with the anticipated loss. Try turning it over by praying: "God, this is too much for me, too much to bear alone; please lift this burden from my heart and shoulders." Relax, keep your heart open, and let go of any attempts to control the situation. See what the universe has in store for you.

9. **Using positive self-talk.** Pay attention to the way you speak to yourself, the mind chatter that seems to never end. Be vigilant in catching the negative thoughts, and reframe them into positive ones. Instead of "I can't handle this," say, "I will get through this; I always do." If I tell myself a certain experience is unbearable, it probably will be. Practice disputing the negativity and you'll become more resilient.

10. **Managing stress.** Check-in with yourself and assess your level of stress. If it's too high, do some relaxation exercises, listen to music, work out, take a hot bath, get a massage, meditate, garden, walk, take a vacation or time off, play with or walk animals, watch funny movies, visit friends, or reconnect with people you like.

11. **Dealing with triggers**. When triggered, if you know a button has been pushed that pulls you back to an earlier time in your life, you will promote resilience if you (a) recognize that you are triggered; (b) check in with reality by saying, "This is now, not then"; and (c) doing whatever works best for you when self-care and self-soothing are needed.

12. **Looking for lessons.** Ask yourself what you can learn from a difficult experience. What are the lessons you could take from a stressful time of life? Be open and make this an opportunity to discover

something new, a better way of being. See yourself as a student of life and a survivor of hardship rather than a victim, and you will build resilience.

13. **Feeling the feelings.** Make friends with your emotions. See them as arrows to guide you. Let them come to the surface, pass through you, and continue out into the universe. The more you feel and release, the less possibility you have of becoming depressed. Think of your feelings as a pressure cooker. If you let the steam out, there is less pressure. It takes energy to hold the pressure in and causes you to close off. Your heart is a valve. Keep it open!

14. **Working through anger and resentments.** As a corollary to feeling the feelings, we must let go of anger and resentment. Don't let them immobilize you by holding on to them. What good does it do you to nurse a grievance? Does it really make you less vulnerable? No, it just closes off your energy and prolongs your suffering. Let it go by deciding to open your heart. Find an outlet, saying what's so to an empty chair, talking it out with the person you resent, writing a letter you would never mail, exercising regularly, or drawing faces on balloons and then popping them. Whatever works!

When I had typhoid, I woke each morning and asked myself, "How can I make this an opportunity to grow and change my life?" Lying in bed for long periods of time, I decided to try a new church and to open myself to what might be coming from God. While I was attending my new church, there was a visiting minister. She gave a moving sermon about growth and openness for our later years in life. Afterward, I went up and asked her if I could work with her. She is a spiritual director (similar to a counselor), and I have been learning from her ever since. With her support, I chose to go back to school and graduated from Seattle University with a post-master's certificate in Transforming Spirituality. I have changed churches, I am exercising more, and I am taking several new classes outside of school regarding dreams and goals I have had for many years. While I wouldn't wish typhoid on anyone, it gave me an opportunity to develop my spiritual side and therefore become more resilient.

Invictus

Out of the night that covers me,
Black as the pit from pole to pole,
I thank whatever gods may be
For my unconquerable soul.

In the fell clutch of circumstance
I have not winced nor cried aloud.
Under the bludgeonings of chance
My head is bloody, but unbowed.

Beyond this place of wrath and tears
Looms but the Horror of the shade,
And yet the menace of the years
Finds and shall find me unafraid.

It matters not how strait the gate,
How charged with punishments the scroll,
I am the master of my fate,
I am the captain of my soul.

—William Ernest Henley

38
Humor Is a Necessity

A clown is like an aspirin, only he works twice as fast.

—Groucho Marx

Humor is just another defense against the universe.

—Mel Brooks

The following joke appeared in the *Farmers Digest*:

> "One day a doctor, a farmer and the president of an HMO arrive at the Pearly Gates. St. Peter hesitates, because heaven is getting kind of full. Finally he tells the doctor, "'You may come in, for you have taken care of the sick in their time of need.'" Then he turns to the farmer and says, "'And you, too, may enter for you have grown food to nourish your fellow man.'" Then St. Peter turns to the HMO executive. "'Well, I guess you can come in too—but only for three days.'"

I've told this one to several friends, and it always gets a good laugh. What makes it funny is that the HMO president gets a taste of his own medicine, no pun intended. What makes our laughter a good coping mechanism is that we release the outrage we feel when we consider our objections to people who administer a health care model that is, in general, uncaring and intrusive.

This ability to let go of pent-up feelings is one of the most mature and effective coping skills in our toolkit for life. Your grandmother knew this was so, researchers have proven it, and you probably learned it a long time ago. Think of a time you enjoyed a really good belly laugh, and recall how it put you in a great mood. Recall the funniest thing you ever experienced, and notice the wonderful feeling that arises. Maybe you're even smiling right now.

Humor can be used for "self-talk" when we face life's adversities. Consider the true story told by Dr. Stan Wilson in his book *Rising Above Shame*. His friend Barbara enters a room where a chess match is in progress, viewed by a small crowd. As always, Barbara wears a longhaired wig to cover large, stress-induced bald spots on her head. Directly over the chessboard is a hanging lamp fixture. Barbara seats herself next to one of the participants and catches her wig on the lamp. By the time she plops down on the couch, the wig is hanging from the lamp for everyone to see. The room freezes in a moment of shared embarrassment, but Barbara chooses not to retrieve the offending hairpiece. Instead, she begins to laugh, and soon, everyone in the room is laughing with her. While I can't say for sure, I imagine Barbara told herself, "Better to laugh at my misfortune than to let it get the best of me." Humor relieved the tension and drew attention from Barbara's moment of humiliation. She proved that when things go wrong, laughter provides a way of coping with difficult feelings.

I just loved the scene in the movie *Mrs. Doubtfire*, where Robin Williams, posing as a grandmotherly woman so he could be with his beloved children, catches the front of his dress on fire while cooking. Instead of falling apart, he recovers by saying, "This must be what hot flashes are like!" He proceeds to take the lids off the pots on the stove and slaps his chest with them to extinguish the fire. The audience, which roared with laughter, could learn from Mrs. Doubtfire's childlike ability to laugh off adversity. And so can we. If you don't already have a good sense of humor, refind the child within you by watching children as they interact and play with one another. By emulating their laughter, you will be certain to improve your physical and mental health.

39
Mindfulness

Try to be mindful, and let things take their course. Then your mind will become still in any surroundings, like a clear forest pool. All kinds of wonderful, rare animals will come to drink at the pool, and you will clearly see the nature of all things. You will see many strange and wonderful things come and go, but you will be still.

—Achaan Chah

If you have picked up this book or ordered it online, chances are you have been dealing with a problem or issue yet to be solved. These problems likely trouble you, compromise your happiness, or perhaps even overwhelm you at times. You may have sought help through counseling, medication management, or other self-help books but didn't receive the relief you seek and deserve. You may have even "self-medicated" with some kind of drug or alcohol or another type of activity like overeating or compulsive sex, gambling, or spending. At times, it may seem like nothing works and you sink into hopelessness and helplessness. At times like these, one of our best coping strategies is to learn and practice mindfulness.

Mindfulness is a way of paying attention to what is happening for you in the present moment. It is a step above ordinary self-awareness in that there is a conscious effort to observe your experience from a distance without being judgmental. If that proves impossible, you can at least recognize when you are adding in a judgment. As an example, I am aware of having a reaction to the person in the car next to me as I realize she is driving and text-messaging at the same time. I think she is a stupid, inconsiderate driver. I am frustrated and angry.

Mindfulness is different. Here, I bring a more complete attention to my experience and at the same time have some distance from it. I may still be aware of my frustration and anger, but I observe that my mind is making a judgment about this woman. I simultaneously notice the tension in my jaw, that my breathing has become shallow, and remember I have on occasion spoken into my cell phone while driving, which isn't that different from what she is doing. So I pay attention, but in a way that is open to what's there, interested in what's there, and accepting of what's there—even if I don't like it! It doesn't mean I'm all peace and love, as I'm concerned about her behavior and entitled to be. I'm just wholly focused on the present moment. I deal with her by giving her a wide berth. If she drives dangerously, I can pull over and call 911 and make a report.

To learn mindfulness, we practice meditation. Here is a sitting meditation, based on the ancient Buddhist principle of *vipassana*, loosely translated as insight. As taught by the Buddha 2,500 years ago, vipassana allows us to transform ourselves by observing our experience, such that we can see things as they really are. It's easy to do, just follow the steps listed here:

1. **Sit comfortably with your feet preferably on the floor to ground your energy.** Keep your spine reasonably straight, allow your shoulders to drop comfortably, and gently fold your hands in your lap.

2. **Close your eyes, and place some attention on your mind** (its thoughts and images) **and some on your body** (its sensations, the sounds it registers).

3. **Using a silent and gentle inner voice, make labels** for your basic experiences in the following ways:
   - If you should happen to notice your mind formulating thoughts in clear or subtle words or sentences, silently say, "Thinking."

- If you should happen to notice a feeling (mad, sad, glad, frightened, excited, jealous, embarrassed, and so on), make the label, "Feeling."
- If you should happen to notice yourself visualizing a mental image of a person, place, object, scene, memory, or fantasy, make the label, "Visualizing."
- When you notice a physical body sensation or register a sound (e.g., tightness in the gut, feet touching the floor, the clock ticking in a room, the cool temperature in your hands, your chest expanding with in-drawn breath, a bird chirping outdoors, fatigue or tension in your forehead, and so on), simply make the label, "Sensing."

4. **Make labels every few seconds.** Try not to get hung up on whether your experiences are positive or negative, pleasant or unpleasant—in other words, try to let go of judgments. If you can't do that, then notice you are judging and label that experience accordingly, "Thinking."

5. **If you cannot decide which label best applies, make an educated guess,** as it doesn't make any difference. You needn't differentiate between different experiences (e.g., moody, sad, glad, worried, ashamed, bored, happy, jealous, frightened); all get the same label, "Feeling."

6. **If you experience periods of time during which there is no experience** of thinking, feeling, visualizing, or sensing (your mind is quiet and peaceful), make the label, "Peace."

7. **Keep making labels with a gentle and accepting voice**, and focus deeply on whatever emerges. *The goal is not to try to get to Peace or return to Peace but merely to notice what is happening and let it be without interference.*

8. **To finish, open your eyes and remain aware,** but without making labels. Take a moment to notice how good it feels to breathe.

Mindfulness takes time and practice. It's just like learning to play the piano. Meditate daily (choose three minutes, five minutes, or twenty minutes), noticing how your experience constantly changes. If you miss a day, no big deal, but try not to miss two days in a row. If you want to meditate twice a day, fine, but don't go longer than thirty minutes per session. Eventually, inner peace will come as a by-product of doing the meditation, but it is not the immediate goal. The goal is to notice your experience and make labels. You will discover you have more equanimity, the quality of remaining calmer and are more even tempered during times of stress. Things that used to bother you will no longer, or they will bother you less. With mindfulness, you are better at coping. You will be watching the movie of your life unfolding versus being lost in the movie and not even knowing you're lost. Life will become easier and more fun.

40
Seed an Epiphany

Stopping in my tracks I turn and face the sun. Bright light filters through the oak and eucalyptus trees rising grandly from the lower side of the hill. Enveloped in warmth, my breathing becomes lighter, more even. I'm taking deep down–through-my-body breaths. Soft, loving breaths. How good I feel just to breathe. Breath is life. How have I not noticed this before? Rooted to the earth, I stretch out my arms and stand like a tree, savoring a rush of energy that streams through my body. I feel a sense of kinship with the old oaks that surround me.

God has always been present for me, but now I am present to God. My heart cracks open, wide open. At first this openness seems more physical than spiritual, as if I'm weightless and airborne in one of my flying dreams. The moment seems timeless, though I want it to last forever. Standing in place, I haven't the slightest conception of what to do next. It's okay, I remind myself. Everything is okay!

—Stanley Wilson

In this quotation from the novel *Stubblefield*, the first-person narrator experiences an epiphany, a sudden and unforeseen manifestation of the meaning of something. Through the epiphany, this young man releases his senseless fears, guilty conscience, and horrific memories—a lifetime of suffering. Though epiphanies are rare and difficult to explain in words, our narrator's epiphany contains all the elements common to such momentous experiences:

- Breathing becomes more natural.
- The body feels grounded yet weightless.
- Rivers of energy stream through the body.
- An intimacy with a Higher Being is felt.

- Inner peace is attainted.
- Time stands still.
- Identification with spirit over mind and body.

Why would I have a chapter on epiphany in a book on developing coping skills? The answer is not an obvious one, but I maintain that everyone is entitled to an experience of Higher Power that is both personal and meaningful. Without such an experience, you will find yourself at a loss when you are most stressed and distressed by the vagaries of life. It doesn't matter if you are a Christian, Jew, Muslim, Buddhist, Sikh, or Sufi; each person has a sense of where to direct such prayers.

A few years ago, I journeyed to Mongolia. My heart was open but heavy, having recently grieved the deaths of several loved ones. I visited a magnificent Buddhist temple in Ulan Bataar, the oldest in Mongolia. Smelling of earth and incense, it quickened my desire for answers about the meaning of death and the direction of my life. A grayish-white vertical prayer stone, well worn and blackened in one spot, clearly indicated the path of those who came before me. As I knelt, I placed my forehead against this spot and offered my question. The surge of a lightning bolt coursed through my body, and I felt the greatest sense of peace I had ever experienced. The answer I received changed the purpose of my life and my perception of the cycle of life in the universe. I realized that even the sun will die; that death is part of life.

To seed clouds, meteorologists sprinkle silver iodide particles in order to produce rain. To seed dreams, the dreamer asks for information during sleep that will enhance his or her life in various ways. The dreamer may request healing imagery, information from the unconscious that will solve a particular problem, or wisdom that will illuminate the nature of the mind. To seed an epiphany, you must sprinkle your consciousness with prayers of petition and positive suggestions to produce the desired experience. Here are all the instructions you'll need:

- Burn a little sage (and sweetgrass and cedar if available) in a clay pot or wooden bowl to help seed your epiphany. This is an ancient

Native American ritual called smudging, a practice that will cleanse your space and your body of any accumulated negative energy.

- Fan the smoke from the burning herbs from head to foot, and then lie quietly in a comfortable position to ensure a rewarding experience.

- Take several deep breaths and notice the rising and falling of your abdomen. Breathe all the way down to your toes, and when it is time to exhale, just let go. There should be no effort on the exhalation.

- If your mind produces thoughts, just let them go without judgment or aversion and return your attention to the sensations of your breathing. This will put your mind in a receptive state and afford you a higher state of consciousness.

- When you feel comfortably relaxed and in a receptive state, pray for an epiphany.

Here are sample prayers, or, if you prefer, you may script your own in accord with your own beliefs and language:

- Dear God, may I be filled with the light of your love and learn the deeper meaning of life.

- Higher Power, I consent to the gift of an epiphany that will reveal the true nature of things.

- Sacred sage, sacred plants, cleanse my body, mind, and spirit and prepare me to receive an epiphany.

If you do reject the existence of a Supreme Being, use your intention. "I ask for an epiphany, knowing my consciousness can produce such a blessing."

After seeding the epiphany, resume your normal activities but notice any significant disruptions to your inner peace. When they occur (this is inevitable), notice the disruption, take a series of deep breaths, and repeat the instructions. If you need to do something to handle the disruption (calm yourself and accept what is happening, remove yourself from a situation that arouses anxiety, express yourself to someone who has intruded on your space, or ask for help in circumstances that overwhelm you), do it mindfully and then return your attention to the sensations of breathing and the seeding of the epiphany.

If you do this with effort and aim for six weeks, you will likely experience an epiphany of your own. If it doesn't happen, stick with it. Your epiphany will certainly come, and life as you know it will never be the same!

I wish I could show you, when you are lonely or in darkness, the Astonishing Light of your own Being.

—Hafiz

41
Something to Fall Back On

The force that created the unimaginable splendors and the unimaginable horrors has taken refuge in us, and it will follow our commands.

—St. Catherine of Siena

Only the snow lions among us can go into solitude in the wilderness and achieve enlightenment alone.

—Tibetan proverb

Lord, make me an instrument of Your Peace.
Where there is hatred, let me sow love;
Where there is injury, pardon;
Where there is doubt, faith;
Where there is despair, hope;
Where there is darkness, light;
And where there is sadness, joy.
O Divine Master, grant that I may not so much seek
To be consoled as to console;
To be understood as to understand;
To be loved as to love;
For it is in giving that we receive;
It is in pardoning that we are pardoned;
And it is in dying that we are born to eternal life.

—St. Francis of Assisi

Sometimes we fall asleep, caught up in the rush of our lives, and then, seemingly out of nowhere, we receive an unexpected wake-up call. This usually comes in the form of a loss—a sudden job change, a serious illness, a painful divorce, or the death of a loved one. It is during these moments of crisis that our usual coping strategies fall short and we need something to fall back on. At times such as these, it is helpful to summon our Highest Self, the self expressed by St. Francis eight hundred years ago in the prayer at the beginning of this chapter.

It is my belief that by reciting this prayer or offering up any heartfelt prayer to our Higher Power, we contact the spiritual being that inhabits all of us and find strength to endure our difficult circumstances. If we can remain an instrument of God's will regardless of what is happening, we will find some measure of comfort no matter how enormous the loss.

As a counselor who has worked in the criminal justice system, I have been witness to some of the awful things people do to other people. It is tempting to judge and hate those who act out and victimize those less powerful. I believed in holding people accountable for the harm they inflicted, but also sought to console and pardon in accord with the words of St. Francis. Without proselytizing any particular religion, I taught the idea that we can always fall back on our Higher Power and turn our lives around no matter how out of control they may seem. This is how I choose to live my life, knowing that every moment is a gift and that I can give back by walking a spiritual path.

The prayer of St. Francis reminds us we are never alone and that we can always connect up with a force too powerful to be fathomed. With this in mind, we can pray and request what we need in order to cope with otherwise overwhelming circumstances. If we are afraid to be alone, we can pray for strength to endure rather than praying for a special person to come into our life. If we are furious with someone whom we believe has mistreated us, we can pray for understanding and forgiveness rather than for God to change or punish the offender. If we are ill, we can pray for healing, but we can also pray for the ability to move through the fear and not allow it to immobilize us. In this way, we ask for liberation rather than the specific outcome we would like.

A Course in Miracles, by Dr. Helen Schucman, tells us, "God is the strength in which I trust." If we choose to rely on our own strength and our own strength alone, we indeed have much to fear. Conversely, if we are humble and wise enough to look to our Higher Power when circumstances overwhelm us, we grow spiritually and discover the true nature of our courage and wisdom. Any ritual that puts you in touch with your spiritual nature and allows you to be receptive to the presence and action of a Higher Power is useful, e.g., attending a church service, lighting candles, meditation, reading religious or spiritual literature, communing with nature, and so on. It matters not if we pray on our knees or standing up, in church or in the checkout line. We can offer up prayers anywhere and anytime and know that a Higher Power is listening to us when we are most in need. Then we truly have something to fall back on. Try it the next time you feel overwhelmed.

To Come Home to Yourself

May all that is unforgiven in you
Be released.

May your fears yield
Their deepest tranquilities.

May all that is unlived in you
Blossom into a future
Graced with love.

—John O'Donohue

Part Two
REACHING YOUR DREAMS
AND GOALS

What would you do if you weren't afraid?
—Unknown

Never give up on a dream just because of the time it will take to accomplish it.
The time will pass anyway.
—Earl Nightingale

When I thought I couldn't go on, I forced myself to keep going.
My success is based on persistence, not luck.
—Estee Lauder

42
Put an End to Procrastination

The best way to get something done is to begin.

—Unknown

Procrastination is the thief of time.

—Edward Young

If you procrastinate, you are not alone.

Feel comforted? Probably not. Your cluttered desk, overdue tax return, and half-finished projects create enough stress and anxiety for ten people. You wilt under the pressure of too many obligations and feel overwhelmed by endless "to-do" lists. What you really need are better ways to manage your time and strategies to develop more efficient work habits. Whether your problem is based on laziness, perfectionism, fear of failure, or attachment to the junk that paralyzes you, the following plan will help you overcome procrastination.

1. **Set out specific and realistic goals, whether the task is large or small.** Write them out, making them very specific.

2. **Evaluate the personal value of your goal(s).** How important is it to you? Is it a priority? Be honest; do you really want to achieve the goal?

3. **Develop a realistic action plan.** Write out the individual steps, and ask yourself if each is doable.

4. **Take small, sequential steps.** Include time, energy, money, and personal limits. If you still feel immobilized, act on it by breaking the steps down into yet smaller, bite-sized pieces.

5. **Tell your friends about your goals.** Making your plan public will help hold you accountable.

6. **Discuss your fears and face them head-on.** Please see chapter 33, "Fear Is No Burden." Enlist a friend to help. Talk about "being stuck," and get support.

7. **Estimate a realistic time frame.** If you fall off your time line, reevaluate and set a new one. Use a calendar to give you a global look at your time frame.

8. **Use success markers.** Write down your achievements, check off the "to-do's" on your list, and celebrate what you've accomplished.

9. **Reward yourself for your successes.** Use positive self-talk: "Job well done!" "Great job! I did it!" "If I can do this, I can do other things, too." Show off your accomplishment to others. Brag a little. Celebrate. Take a hot bath, go for a fun hike, or enjoy your favorite restaurant.

The following case is an example. Steve, a successful professional and world-class procrastinator, had accumulated a mountain of clutter on every surface of his large, old-fashioned oak desk. He always intended to clean up the mess but put it off because the job looked daunting. In the middle of a business meeting, a three-foot stack of papers and magazines toppled like an avalanche, embarrassing him in front of his peers. Only then did he resolve to take action.

Using the plan outlined in this chapter, Steve wrote out a realistic goal: file or discard not less than ten pieces of paper every working day. He e-mailed his friends about his intentions and stuck to it. Some days, he would feel inspired and do up to fifty pieces. He also asked a well-organized friend if she could help. She suggested recycling the entire stack of business journals he'd decided to save because he would probably never get around to reading them. In less than two months, his desk was clear, and after rewarding himself with a massage and a round of golf, he set his sights on his disorganized bookshelves.

Stop saying, "I wish," start saying, "I will."

—Unknown

You are never too old to set another goal or to dream a new dream...

—C.S. Lewis

Put an End to Procrastination Worksheet

Evaluate and List Goal(s):

_____

_____

_____

_____

_____

Action Plan/Time Frame:

1._____
2._____
3._____
4._____
5._____
6._____
7._____

Small Steps:

1._____
2._____
3._____
4._____
5._____
6._____
7._____

Fears:

1._____
2._____
3._____
4._____
5._____
6._____
7._____

Plan for Attending to Fears:

1._____
2._____
3._____
4._____
5._____
6._____
7._____

Build Support System/Meeting Times:

1._____
2._____
3._____
4._____
5._____
6._____
7._____

Self-Talk:

1._____
2._____
3._____
4._____
5._____
6._____
7._____

Success Markers:

1._____
2._____
3._____
4._____
5._____
6._____
7._____

Rewards:

1._____
2._____
3._____
4._____
5._____
6._____
7._____

Dream it, wish it, do it.

—Unknown

43
Is Being Late a Problem?

People count the faults of those who keep them waiting.

—French Proverb

Unfaithfulness in the keeping of an appointment is an act of clear dishonesty. You may as well borrow a person's money as his time.

—Horace Mann

Jane had an ongoing problem with chronic lateness. It affected her friendships, her business relationships, and pretty much every time commitment she made. She was so late to an important appointment with a client that the client left in a huff. A painter who showed up to paint several rooms of her home waited for over an hour before leaving. He refused to come back, as it was the second time she'd stood him up. Her own children would set a time to meet with her and then show up a half hour late, knowing she still wouldn't be there. Friendships had been lost because she'd repeatedly set times to meet for a movie, luncheon, or other plans and would be grossly late. Anxious, depressed, and increasingly feeling isolated, Jane came to therapy and reported she had hit bottom and wanted to work on her problem.

Let's first explore several of the reasons people are chronically late. This isn't the person who gets hung up in traffic or called to an unexpected meeting; it's the one who is predictably late because it's a pattern. Lateness may be your problem, or it may a problem for someone you have to deal with on a regular basis. Here are eleven of the most likely possibilities:

1. **Attention Deficit Disorder (ADD).** ADD is not just a problem with willpower or an excuse for zoning out; it is a no-fault brain disorder

that affects the chemistry and wiring of the brain. People with ADD are often unfocused, disorganized, and forgetful. These all lead to chronic lateness, forgetting appointments, and missing deadlines. Add in poor listening skills, ill-fated attempts at multitasking, and losing track of time, and you can imagine how difficult it is for ADD sufferers to be punctual.

2. **Poor Time Management.** Some people, and not just those with ADD, do not manage time well. They never learned to use a calendar and may overrely on memory to keep their schedule and commitments straight. These chronically late folks are often poor judges of how long things realistically take. They will allow thirty minutes in rush-hour traffic to arrive at a destination that is more likely to be ninety minutes away.

3. **Narcissism.** Consider the characteristics of the narcissist. Narcissists are typically self-oriented, seemingly incapable of empathy, rich in feelings of entitlement, willing to take advantage of others, unable to see things from another's perspective, and lacking in terms of self-awareness. Given this list of traits, it is a wonder that a narcissist is ever on time. God bless them, these brothers and sisters are more important than the rest of us, so being late is our problem, not theirs.

4. **Passive-Aggression.** Chronic lateness is sometimes a type of passive-aggressive behavior; that is, the late person is expressing aggression or hostility in an indirect or nonassertive way. If you ask your passive-aggressive husband to be at the fundraiser no later than 7:00 p.m., he may intentionally be late as a way to feel in control or to punish you. You tell your rebellious teenage daughter to be available for after-school pickup at a certain time, as you have to return to work, and she is never on time. She is essentially saying, "Screw you!" via her chronic lateness.

5. **Mental Health Issues.** Depression often robs people of their energy and motivation. They become helpless and hopeless, so being late

happens because they simply don't have the investment or drive to be on time. It doesn't matter because nothing matters. Anxiety and worry can sap a person's energy or vitality and make it difficult to meet time commitments. Instead of focusing on being on time, anxious people are preoccupied with what could go wrong. When they should be planning to be somewhere on time, they get caught up in their "home movies," and by that, I mean the ones they play in their heads where they imagine catastrophes. There can be other mental health issues that can cause people not to be organized or operate in reality. If this is the case, it will affect being late.

6. **Drug and/or Alcohol Problems.** You have a drug or alcohol problem if your drinking causes family conflict, if it interferes with your work, if it potentially jeopardizes your health, or if it has or could get you in trouble with the law. This definition avoids debating about alcoholism or addiction. Lots of clients will argue they are not alcoholic, but because they have had two DUIs or because they are sometimes too hungover to go to work, they will admit to having a problem. That problem is also a common cause for people to procrastinate, ignore, forget, or be chronically late for appointments and other responsibilities.

7. **Poor Social Skills.** Sometimes those who are chronically late are not ADD, passive-aggressive, or experiencing any of the other reasons—they simply lack the social awareness that being on time is the proper thing to do. This may be a combination of not being self-smart or not being people-smart and coming across as inconsiderate and ignorant of social convention. Often, these folks had poor role models when it comes to punctuality.

8. **Living in Chaos.** Chronic lateness is sometimes a reflection of a life that is characterized by disorder and confusion. The person's daily activities are so chaotic he or she is simply unable to honor time commitments. I've had any number of clients who lived in clutter and could never remember where they put their appointment card.

Even if they called for a reminder, it was iffy whether they would show up on time or at all.

9. **Overcommitment.** Some people have so much going on and so little time to accomplish all their responsibilities that it translates into lateness. A problem that compounds being overly committed is that such persons have difficulty saying "no" or setting boundaries, so they keep taking on more and more. Yes, these people are often very compassionate, but they are also unable to set limits. "Want to organize the Girl Scouts' yearly camping trip?" "Sure." "We need someone to volunteer for the PTA bake sale." "Of course." Only now they can't get to work on time because they're burned out and bone tired.

10. **Not Being Grounded.** People who are grounded are well-balanced and sensible. When you're not, you come across as disconnected or even flaky. To be current or on time, you need to be grounded and operating in reality. It's hard to be aware of others around you and their time expectations if you've checked out or are numb.

11. **Cognitive Impairment.** Some people are late because they are not thinking clearly, because of poor judgment or because of memory problems. These cognitive difficulties can be due to aging, head injury, seizure disorders, early dementia, or a host of other causes. Chronic lateness should sometimes result in a trip to the neurologist and not just for the elderly.

Here are some helpful hints if you find yourself struggling with one or more of the reasons for chronic lateness. Make a plan for the eventual solution.

- Be honest with yourself. Identify the problem, and take responsibility for turning it around.

- Being on time is expected in our society. Be aware that this is how to keep friends, show respect, and be successful at work, school, and any other endeavor you wish to achieve.

- Get a calendar, and write down your commitment times.

- Carry the calendar with you, and put it on your nightstand at night.

- Review the calendar before you go to bed, and plan for the next day.

- Read your calendar when you get up in the morning, and plan your day.

- If necessary, get a calendar with an alarm that will remind you of your appointments.

- If you suspect you have ADD, get an evaluation, treatment, or medication.

- Be realistic about how many commitments you can take on in a day without being late or rushing to get to them.

- If you are a slow riser in the morning, make the appointment later in the day. If you're slow coming back from lunch, make the appointment later in the afternoon. If you get tired in the afternoons, make the appointment earlier in the day.

- If you use your lateness to express hostility, find a more assertive, direct, and mature way to express it. If you don't know how to do that, seek out a counselor.

- If, in your most honest and private moments, you will admit to being narcissistic or having such tendencies, you must get professional help. This is one problem you cannot handle on your own. You have been emotionally injured, but adopting an attitude of entitlement will only make matters worse.

- If your lateness is a function of a mental health, drug, or alcohol problem, seek support from others, including professionals. Be honest in assessing yourself.

- Do not be afraid to arrive at the appointment early. Have something with you that you can work on—a good book, a device for checking your e-mail or to play games on (like a smartphone), something to write on, or a list to go over, or you could close your eyes and meditate.

- Leave a bit early to give yourself a buffer. Have a realistic plan that factors in what time of day it is and allows for unexpected things to come up, like traffic or parking problems.

- If you're living in chaos, get help in order to get clearer and more organized. Avoid involvement with people who operate in crisis mode. It's contagious. Consider counseling or hiring a life coach.

- Learn to say "no" and make a counteroffer (for example: "I'm very interested in what you are saying; however, I need to set another time with you to talk about this or I'll be late to my next appointment."). If you are unable to set limits with yourself or others, seek professional help.

- Ask yourself if you're grounded. Some of the cues when you are not grounded are: feeling fear/anxiety, not being physically-coordinated and tripping or bumping into things, friends telling you that you are flaky, and not being well-organized or focused. Have you taken your medication? Have you eaten? Are you hydrated? If not, then do so. Other helpful tips are exercising, gardening, practicing Yoga, doing meditation, learning to breathe in a mindful way, listening to soothing music, petting an animal, using a touchstone, or practicing a time-proved exercise that helps you to get grounded and stay focused. If you have trouble following through on this see chapter 29, "Are You Grounded?" or seek professional help.

If you want to be punctual, you need to change your behavior and make realistic time commitments. Insanity is repeating the same thing and expecting a different outcome. In summary, if you slip, do another fearless inventory of yourself and go through the list again. Don't give up. Keep at it until you get it right.

44
Scattered or Overwhelmed?

Being in control of your life and having realistic expectations about your day-to-day challenges are the keys to stress management, which is perhaps the most important ingredient to living a happy, healthy, rewarding life.

—Marilu Henner

Sometimes we take on too much and put ourselves under extraordinary stress, either out of necessity or because we have trouble saying "no" to others. I see people who act as if there are forty-eight hours in a day or perhaps they think they have a clone. Others seem driven by unconscious forces; namely, they overcommit because their self-worth comes from doing things well or because they are simply afraid that if they don't overfunction, they will be unappreciated and abandoned. Whatever the reason, these poor souls end up under continual time pressure and committed to too many projects and responsibilities. If any part of this problem resonates with you, you may find yourself feeling scattered, overwhelmed, overcommitted and sliding into burnout.

Marianne, a client in her late forties, has a high-powered job and a six-figure income. She feels beholden to the technology company that writes her paychecks. She takes on way too much. The company culture dictates that salaried employees are expected to work sixty- to seventy-hour weeks. Marianne can handle this (I couldn't; I think it's crazy), but in addition to her long hours at work, she has a thirty-minute commute each way and then gets up in the middle of the night and checks cell phone messages and e-mails on her computer. Crazier yet, she will actually reply to e-mail messages at all hours of the night. Ready for the kicker? Marianne has two children and is a Girl Scout den mother for her eldest daughter. Forget that she complains about being scattered and overwhelmed; that's the least of her worries. Marianne is working herself into an early grave.

Let's discuss some interventions we made in Marianne's life, and then I'll give you four simple questions to help you deal with taking on too much. First, Marianne agreed to devote five minutes in the morning, five minutes at noon, and five minutes in the evening to doing an emotional check-in with herself. The purpose of the check-in was to determine how stressed she was and assess early signs of burnout (see chapter 46, "Taking On Too Much"). Second, she consented, reluctantly, not to check the phone or computer in the middle of the night. If she fudged, she had to make a fifty-dollar charitable contribution to the nonprofit of her choice—an ordeal that helped her stay accountable to the goal. Third, before she made any kind of commitment or took on any kind of new project, she had to take twenty-four hours to think it over. This helped her get away from automatically agreeing to do everything asked of her, a lifelong bad habit. She also agreed to consider how long a commitment would take, how complicated it was, how much time pressure it came with, and how important it was to her. Lastly, Marianne agreed to devote not less than one hour before bed to "me" time, allowing her to relax, read, watch television, listen to music, meditate, pray, work out, burn candles, take warm baths, or do whatever she wanted without interruption (her husband, who was worried about Marianne's pace of life, happily took on the task of running interference for her).

Finally, Marianne was instructed to ask herself the following questions whenever she found herself dealing with one of her accepted commitments:

Now: Does this have to be done right now?

Later: Could this wait an hour, a day, a week, or a month?

Delegate: Can this be delegated to another?

Not at All: Even though ideally I would like to do it, is this really necessary?

Feeling overwhelmed, ask yourself: "Now, Later, Delegate, Not at All?" Someone once said, "Enlightenment comes from subtraction." So does stress management.

I'm pleased to report that Marianne has simplified her life. Paradoxically, by taking on less, she claims she actually gets more done, and at the same time, she has more energy for herself and her family. No one at work has noticed she has changed her routine or her habits, or, if they have, they have not commented.

Clutter is not just stuff on your floor—it's anything that stands between you and the life you want to be living.

—Peter Walsh

Scattered or Overwhelmed? Worksheet

Make a daily list using these four categories. Write tasks under each category. This is a proven method of prioritizing tasks, so they won't overwhelm you. A manageable life is a happier life.

Now	Later	Delegate	Not at All
1. _____	_____	_____	_____
_____	_____	_____	_____
2. _____	_____	_____	_____
_____	_____	_____	_____
3. _____	_____	_____	_____
_____	_____	_____	_____
4. _____	_____	_____	_____
_____	_____	_____	_____
5. _____	_____	_____	_____
_____	_____	_____	_____
6. _____	_____	_____	_____
_____	_____	_____	_____
7. _____	_____	_____	_____
_____	_____	_____	_____

45
Why Delegate?

Delegating work works, provided the one delegating works, too.

—Robert Half

With one ass, you can't dance in two weddings.

—Yiddish Proverb

Judy, a single mother with two teenage children, felt overwhelmed by the challenge of balancing work and family. No matter how hard she tried, she found herself unable to get a handle on things. She had her own bookkeeping business and wanted to expand to meet the needs of a growing clientele, but she just couldn't keep up. She slept poorly, ate irresponsibly, and felt exhausted by the end of the day.

Like many working moms, Judy struggled with guilt for not spending enough time with the kids. The house was a mess. Her life was a mess. A perfectionist, she couldn't let go of things and believed she had to do everything herself or it wouldn't get done properly. Stress overwhelmed her, and her body kept score. Her stomach ached constantly, and her beautiful hair (one of Judy's best assets) was falling out in clumps. Finally, her emotional pain and physical deterioration caused her to seek counseling.

After a few sessions to identify the problem, Judy agreed she must learn to let go of trying to control everything and delegate whenever possible. She hired a new staff member (with careful scrutiny) who could lighten her workload. She also hired a housekeeper with the same diligence, a woman who could relieve her of certain time-consuming household duties. In addition, Judy outlined expectations for each of her children as to what they would do to help her keep the home tidy. If the kids chose not to comply with her reasonable demands, she would not argue; she would simply relieve them of their cellphone and computer privileges. Amazing what teens will do to keep the things they covet!

Delegation, simply put, is entrusting responsibilities to others, including decision-making. It involves coaching up other people to a certain level of skill rather than just dumping tasks in their laps. By delegating to the right person, you can greatly reduce your stress and improve your own productivity. It frees you up to maximize your own time, energy, and knowledge. Moreover, it increases time available to do more things, such as planning, strategizing, and dreaming up and implementing new personal or professional opportunities.

Trying to do everything that needs to be done is grandiose and makes no sense. Good delegation follows the steps above and will reduce your stress. It will enable you to save time, reach your goals, and preserve your sanity. It increases productivity in the workplace and at home. Just ask Judy. After learning to delegate, she is now moving forward with her business plans, has more time to be with her children, and has her house clean and well-organized. She is eating healthy food and taking supplements prescribed by a naturopath. Her hair has grown back, and her sleep has improved immeasurably. By letting go of control, she has regained control (to the extent we are ever "in control").

A Short Course on How to Delegate

1. **Set aside your ego.** You're not the only one who can do the things you need done.

2. **Acknowledge when you need to delegate.** Smart people know when they're overwhelmed and need help.

3. **Pick tasks to delegate.** Focus especially on the time-consuming ones that don't require a high level of expertise.

4. **Ask for help, or go get it.** Don't wait for volunteers or others to anticipate what you need.

5. **Collect information.** Check out the person who will do the task, and get references.

6. **Communicate clearly.** Be clear about the tasks you need done, and train the person according to reasonable standards.

7. **Motivate and praise.** Encourage the person who is doing the task.

8. **Review periodically.** Attend to how tasks are being done. Be patient with mistakes.

9. **Have clear boundaries.** Define the boundary regarding the relationship with the person to whom you've delegated.

10. **Have a backup plan.** Switch to Plan B if things go sour. Learn as much as you can from your prior experience. Find another resource to delegate to.

46
Taking On Too Much
(Prescription for Burnout)

Burnout is nature's way of telling you, you've been going through the motions and your soul has departed; you're a zombie, a member of the walking dead, a sleepwalker.

—Sam Keen

Burnout can happen when we get exposed to too much stress for too long a time, usually in the workplace. We then begin to feel overwhelmed and exhausted. When you burn out, your energy plummets and you lose interest in whatever task is at hand. Burnout saps your energy and reduces your productivity, leaving you drained, helpless, hopeless, trapped, irritable, and cynical. Victims of burnout are pretty unhappy people and often resort to escapist behaviors, such as alcohol or drug abuse, compulsive sex or spending. Needless to say, burning out will eventually jeopardize your job, personal life, and physical health.

Burnout doesn't usually sneak up on you, which means you have time to recognize its early signs and ward it off. To avoid burnout, put to use the following suggestions:

1. **Know your physical and emotional limits.** Know how much is too much in everything you do, including work, activities, weekends, and vacations. Don't put more effort into a project than you have time for recovery. Use a day planner or a weekly calendar to monitor how many obligations you're taking on. Remember, a limita-

tion is a *limitation*, not a weakness, and knowing your limitations is a strength!

2. **If you don't know your limits, gather information.** Find out how much you can take on and still maintain a sense of physical and emotional health. Experiment with doing a little more than usual, and then back off. Be mindful of your age, health, current circumstances, and overall stress level.

3. **Attend to cues that signal danger.** Often, these will be physical symptoms, such as stomachaches, headaches, neck and back pain, or stress-induced hair loss. They may also be psychological, such as having difficulty concentrating or feeling driven, trapped, and resentful. They may also be spiritual if you're feeling despair and not connected to your Higher Power.

4. **Get good and get comfortable with saying, "No!"** If a difficult boss is giving you more than you can handle, speak up. Set up a meeting to discuss the conditions that will maximize your productivity.

5. **Leave work on time, and don't take work home.** Learn to prioritize and stay organized. When you get home, do something relaxing, such as walking the dog, listening to soft music, reading a good book, or viewing a funny movie. Give yourself time to shift gears.

6. **Take a vacation.** Want to get away? Just do it! Take your dream vacation, and leave work behind. Make a deal with yourself and if you have a travel partner to avoid any discussions of whatever it was that burned you out. One of the best ways to manage depression or stress is to have vacations to look forward to.

Taking On Too Much (Prescription for Burnout) Worksheet

1. **Present life stressors** (extra duties at work, death in the family, and so on):

   _____
   _____
   _____
   _____

2. **Personal cues for burnout:**

   a. **Physical** (exhaustion, backaches, nausea, and so on):

   _____
   _____

   b. **Emotional** (feeling helpless, irritable, cynical, and so on):

   _____
   _____

   c. **Thinking** (negative and obsessive thoughts, feeling trapped, and so on):

   _____
   _____

   d. **Addictions** (relapse eating, drinking, gambling, and so on):

   _____
   _____

    e. Spiritually Disconnected (depression, despair, and so on):

_____

_____

3. **How much can I do today and still feel good?** _____

_____

_____

4. **Self-talk** (What responsibilities can I eliminate and delegate?):_____

_____

_____

5. **Ways to say "No":**

_____

_____

6. **Plan and take ongoing vacations:** _____

_____

_____

_____

47
Collecting Information Based on Reality

Question reality, especially if it contradicts the evidence of your hopes and dreams.

—Robert Brault

One of the most important life skills you can learn is to collect information based on reality. Having this skill can make a difference in regards to having a successful career or a healthy relationship, feeling good about yourself, and meeting your goals and dreams without setting yourself up for failure. Some people go through life with one failure after another because they didn't do a good job collecting their information. Being reality-based is essential if you are to make good decisions. Operating in reality is the number-one way to protect yourself and complete your dreams and goals. Only when you're in reality can you make healthy choices, arrive at correct judgments, effectively problem-solve, or step back from a potentially dangerous situation.

Avoid collecting information when you're drinking, drugging, not grounded, depressed, angry, fearful, or upset. All of these throw off your radar and may put you in harm's way. These issues can cause you to make a poor decision. If you doubt yourself and question whether your information is real, it is best to do reality checks with people you respect and who have your best interests at heart. Don't be afraid to look information up on the Internet, read, go back to school, get counseling, talk to your minister, and beam up prayers and ask for direction.

If your Inner Adult is off duty or offline while you're trying to collect information, then there is a strong possibility you are not in reality. Make sure your Inner Child is not masquerading as the Adult when you're collecting information. Pay close attention to cues that suggest your Inner Child might be running the show. When I have the feeling of "energized insistence," I am quite certain it is my Child part who wants to be in charge. If I feel impulsive, impatient, overly eager to come to a decision, or in too big a hurry or have too much energy on the issue, then I'm in my Inner Child. This is the time to wait and see, to summon a more mature Adult part of my personality to take over. This is the time to slow down and decide to collect more information on the subject after I'm in my Adult and grounded in reality.

Here is a useful list to help you develop the ability to collect information based on reality:

1. **Get clear on the issue,** whether it's choosing a boyfriend, partner, or husband; taking a trip; accepting a job; returning to school; or terminating a pregnancy or carrying one to term. Talk about it, write about it, read about it, meditate on it, and pray on it.

2. **Make certain you're in your Inner Adult.** Calm down, center yourself, get support, and take your time to collect the information you need from healthy, functional people who have your best interests in mind.

3. **Watch for cues that you may be coming from your Inner Child.** Do you feel overly excited, silly, impatient, or energized? Are you suffering from denial, amnesia, or "jumping hormones?"

4. **Attend to your intuition.** Does your choice, judgment, or solution give you a "funny" or uncomfortable feeling in your gut? If so, figure out what your body is trying to tell you. Remember, the only time your intuition doesn't work is when you're not using it.

5. **Be drug and alcohol-free when collecting information.** Sober decisions are not always correct, but they have a much higher chance of being so.

6. **Do not be acting out any addictions when making decisions.** I refer to chemical dependency, gambling, overspending, and so on.

7. **Avail yourself to your resources.** Ask for help from healthy friends, family, counselors, ministers, and life coaches. Sit down and read, write, or browse the Internet, and attend classes.

8. **Be brutally honest with yourself.** If you find you are hiding information from the people you know, you're more than likely in your Child part and about to do something you should not be doing.

9. **Ask yourself, "Is this going to hurt me or anyone else?"** If so, take a closer look.

10. **If you are inclined to be manic or unstable, get yourself stabilized** before making decisions or acting on your dreams and goals. Get help from a professional and make sure to take your medication as prescribed.

11. **Are you lonely?** Don't let this be the reason you are choosing to be in a relationship. The reality is if you settle you will then suffer more than the suffering of loneliness.

12. **Ask God, pray, meditate, exercise, be in nature, or seek a source** that will help you to be centered and calm when you're gathering information.

13. **Practice supportive self-talk** when managing yourself around this issue. Examples include:
    - "I need to wait. I can't gather all this information at once."
    - "I need to work out the steps of doing this. I can make a list and do one at a time."
    - "Why am I in such a hurry?"

- "I'm afraid I'm about to do something I'll regret. I have to stop and think this through."
- "I don't need to let my fear be my guide or stop me. I need to find out if the fears are real. If they are real, I'll collect information about what I should do about them."
- "I need to center myself. I can't collect real or reliable information until I do."
- "Maybe I need a second or third or fourth opinion. For whatever reason, I don't trust myself right now."
- "I'm feeling so excited and impulsive. This feels like my Child part!"
- "That funny feeling in my gut is telling me something is amiss. I need to slow down and be sure I'm in reality."

This kind of honest and positive self-talk can ground you in reality and ensure that your judgments, decisions, and solutions have a better chance of success. By keeping an eye out for your Inner Child and summoning your Adult part to handle these important situations, you will protect yourself from many moments of failure, suffering, and potential danger.

A moment of patience may ward off great disaster.
A moment of impatience may ruin a whole life.

—Chinese proverb

48
An Unfair World
(The Dragonfly Story)

God, grant me the Serenity to accept the things I cannot change, Courage to change the things I can, and Wisdom to know the difference.

—Reinhold Niebuhr

When we're children and something happens that seems unfair, it provides an opportunity for parents to teach the skill of handling life's unfairness. If this skill isn't properly learned, we can grow up but find ourselves stuck on fairness issues for an endless period of time. Here is a story I tell my clients if they haven't yet learned the unfairness skill, which is really an acceptance of reality.

When my daughter was in second grade, she caught a beautiful dragonfly from our pond on the farm. She took it to school for "show-and-tell." After school, she brought it home to set it free and two boys took it from her and killed it. Sobbing, she said, "The dragonfly didn't do anything to deserve to be killed. Why do unfair things have to happen?" She went on to say it was "…like war, that people get killed for no reason. These people did nothing wrong. Why can't there be peace?" She cried again.

I rocked and held her until she stopped. I then said, "Unfair things happen. It's part of life. We can't control it. But what we can do is look for the opportunities for what we can do."

She responded, "How will I know when there's an opportunity?"

I said, "You will *know*. It'll be in your power to do something that makes a difference."

A week later, we were walking down the sidewalk in our small rural town. The temperature was approaching one hundred degrees. The storefronts were cheered up with colorful flowers in whiskey barrels on either side of the entryways.

My daughter yelled, "I know what it is!"

I jumped back, thinking perhaps she'd been struck by something.

Excitedly, she added, "This is the opportunity!" She pointed to a black beetle on the sidewalk, belly up, legs wriggling. "I can put this beetle in one of the whiskey barrels in the cool soil under the shade of the flowers. I can't stop it from dying, but I can give it a dignified bug death, or it can recover and go on with its life."

I felt a measure of relief in knowing she was now equipped to deal with the inevitable unfairness of life.

49
Can Humility and Confidence Exist Simultaneously?

If I am not for myself who will be for me. If I am only for myself what am I. If not now? When?

—Rabbi Hillel

Many of my clients struggle with self-esteem issues. Deep down, they suspect they are defective, inadequate, and unlovable—not enough in some way. Some believe that to trust in themselves or have confidence in their own abilities is to be a braggart or be full of themselves. Early in life, they were taught to disavow their own intelligence or talents, and they bought in to this faulty message. This is especially true for girls and young women. Needless to say, such messages have undermined their healthy self-esteem, which, in turn, makes it difficult for them to realize their dreams and goals.

Susan came in to see me because she struggled with believing in herself and realizing her innermost dream. She aspired to become a massage therapist but feared she lacked the intelligence and the ability to become competent in this demanding job. She was convinced she would be unable to learn and retain the medical information necessary to pass a certification test.

Surprisingly, Susan gave a history of being a college graduate and had held down a difficult job in the area of social work. We looked at this and realized she had accomplished a great deal without giving herself credit for it. I suggested she do a reality check and acknowledge she was more capable than she had come to believe. I also asked her to accept that it was normal for her to have some fears while transitioning to a new career. For instance, was this the work she really wanted? Would she be able to sustain a passion for doing massages all day? Would the physical and energetic demands of the job wear out her body?

I encouraged her to let in the fact that she had been able to learn new information in the past and that she had accomplished other academic and career goals. Her confidence grew, and Susan was able to act upon her dream without giving in to self-doubt. It helped her to operate in reality with confidence but also with the humility that comes from accepting that she would not know everything or be the perfect student. This meant she could be open to learning and accepting of the mistakes she would make along the way, something that goes along with starting a second career.

Susan started school for her new profession after collecting information about the expense of becoming a massage therapist and her future earning power. She set a goal of how much she wanted to earn and devised a plan to determine whether this was realistic. She did her homework by interviewing massage therapists already in practice and finding out how difficult it was to find part- versus full-time work after graduation. She also asked important questions about long-term job satisfaction and the physical demands of providing massage for clients who were often injured or in pain.

Susan learned that having confidence made a big difference in her moving forward. When she was stuck in low self-esteem, she made excuses for not pursuing her dreams. She also became aware that she could feel *competent* and *humble* at the same time—that, in fact, the more she knew, the more she realized there was much she didn't know. It reminds me of a saying, "Those who know don't know; those who don't know know!" I think the true professionals are those who don't claim to know it all and who are still open to learning.

Susan was a delight to work with, especially seeing her in possession of the new abilities as a licensed massage therapist. She took responsibility for making her dream happen and now works in a field where she alleviates suffering. She lives more consciously as a health-care professional, and her calling gives her a sense of purpose. Does it mean she is full of herself? No, she is full of self-confidence and full of humility. They work best in tandem.

50
Keep Your Dreams Alive

Our deepest fear is not that we are inadequate. Our deepest fear is that we are powerful beyond measure. It is our light, not our darkness that most frightens us. We ask ourselves, who am I to be brilliant, gorgeous, talented and fabulous? Actually, who are you not to be?

— Marianne Williamson

The future belongs to those who believe in the beauty of their dreams.

—Eleanor Roosevelt

Everyone has dreams, some longed-for aspiration or lofty achievement. It could be to run a marathon, build a dream home, manage a successful business from home, complete a college education, or set sail on a Mediterranean cruise with a loved one.

How is it that some people accomplish such dreams while others stray from the path and wonder what happened? Why do some make their dreams come true while others become complacent, only to end up feeling frustrated, negative, and cynical? To answer these questions, we must ask a more pertinent question: Who determines if such a dream is realized or if it falls by the wayside? The answer is *you*.

Joseph Campbell, the great American mythologist, lecturer, and writer, admonished people to "follow your bliss." He derived this idea from the Upanishads, the nearly three-thousand-year-old texts that form the core of Hindu philosophy (interestingly, these treatises also introduced the ideas of meditation, Yoga, karma, and reincarnation). To Campbell, the idea of following one's bliss was more than a mantra; it was a guide that would both energize and keep one on the right track. To me, Campbell's famous phrase inspires me to dream up whatever it is that will both excite me and make my life more meaningful. Identifying and seeking our bliss is how we keep our dreams alive.

Carol, a fellow mental health professional in her mid-forties, dreamed of writing a book and getting it published. She began writing as a younger woman but bogged down. However, she held on to her desire and began to "pick the brains" of several successful authors, who encouraged her to try again. She joined a writer's group and took a class. "Writers write," her instructor advised, and she began to write for an hour every day. Carol told herself, "I can do this. I *will* do this!" Twenty years after her first start, she sent ten publishing companies a manuscript for a self-help book. The first nine rejected her, and her hopes sagged, but the tenth signed on. The book obtained excellent reviews and sold out ten thousand copies. It is now in its second printing and very much in demand.

Carol has now written and published two more books, and a fourth is being submitted for publication. When asked how she realized her dream, she advises others to "follow your bliss." I agree but believe there is a method to it. We put our heads together and broke down the method into the following ten steps:

1. **You must entertain a burning desire for your dream.** If you're only lukewarm about publishing that poem or running with the bulls in Pamplona, it's not likely to happen.

2. **Commit to your dream by writing it down.** Remember to express your dream in a positive way (for example, "I will purchase a condo in the city" is much more powerful than "I don't want to be a renter forever").

3. **Make a plan for bringing the dream to reality, and visualize yourself living it.** If your dream is to move to a warmer climate, see yourself enveloped in sun on a white sandy beach.

4. **Create action steps, set a time line, and write them down.** In the warmer clime example, you could write: "I will visit and check out Phoenix and San Diego in the next twelve months."

5. **Spend time with friends who are supportive of your dream.** It's easier to realize dreams with the support of others.

6. **Find advisors/mentors who will help you make your dreams a reality.** Use them as guides and a cheering section every step along the way. Making dreams come true requires support.

7. **Create an environment that inspires you in the direction of your dreams.** This may include good books, great music, just the right lighting, and a meditative space like a garden or pond. If you lack such an environment, go regularly to spaces that can do the same thing—gardens, parks, museums, natural settings, art studios, or the library.

8. **Adopt a spiritual philosophy that keeps you going when the going gets tough.** Most likely, you will hit some bumps in the road. This will keep you centered so you can keep your eyes on the prize.

9. **Practice positive self-talk.** "I only have this life to live. I want to make it as meaningful and fulfilling as possible." "How do I wish to spend my life in accordance with my most cherished dreams?" "No matter how long it takes it will happen, as long as I do not quit."

10. **Check your progress regularly.** If you're stuck, figure out why and make the appropriate changes. Perhaps your dream is unrealistic ("I want to travel in outer space" (it's not impossible, just unrealistic)), or you're losing your desire because of a few setbacks then get inspiration from others, classes, reading, or other ideas. If the steps you've outlined are too big, break them down into smaller steps.

These steps are deceptively simple, but they are powerful. Give them a try and see if they work for you. Do you dare make your dreams come true?

Life is too short to be living somebody else's dream.

—Hugh Hefner

All our dreams can come true if we have the courage to pursue them.

—Walt Disney

51
Achieving Goals—The Art of Calculated Risk

And the day came when the risk it took to remain tightly closed in a bud was more painful than the risk it took to bloom.

—Anais Nin

It seems to be a law of nature, inflexible and exorable, that those who will not risk cannot win.

—John Paul Jones

Success is to be measured not so much by the position that one has reached in life, as by the obstacles that one has overcome while trying to succeed.

—Booker T. Washington

Patti, divorced for two years and barely able to make ends meet, felt immobilized by fear. A mother of three grown daughters, she had never worked outside the home and had no self-confidence apart from being a parent. Despite some misgivings, she interviewed for several nanny positions but came across poorly as a result of extreme nervousness. She also applied for minimum-wage jobs at local day-care centers, but her heart wasn't in it and she never took a position. "The truth is," she explained in an apologetic manner, "I don't have any passion for raising other people's children."

I asked the obvious question. "What *is* your passion?"

Her answer came as a surprise. It turned out Patti had a green thumb and spent hours every day puttering in her garden. She would come alive as she talked about planting and cultivating her many varieties of shrubs, trees, annuals, and perennials, as well as harvesting food from her vegetable and herb gardens. At my request, she brought in a series of photos that demonstrated an obvious gift for creative landscaping and gardening. When I wondered aloud why she hadn't applied at any of the many nurseries in our area, Patti simply deflated. Again, it was a confidence problem. She had convinced herself her mind would go blank if a customer asked even the simplest question. She feared she'd have to work a cash register or compute a discount on the calculator and wouldn't have the basic math skills. Minimizing her encyclopedic knowledge of plants and gardens, she even questioned whether she would have anything to offer.

Patti and I took several sessions to explore her fears and develop a plan for productive, gainful employment. We pretty much followed the twelve suggestions below to enhance her potential for success.

1. **Give yourself permission to dream.** Dreaming stimulates creative, powerful ideas. Translate your dreams into realistic goals, and go for it. Read, take classes, and interview others who have successfully achieved similar goals. Patti agreed to put in a request to the universe: "I want to work and be successful at a local nursery."

2. **Develop skill sets.** If you don't yet have the right skills, go get them! Avail yourself to mentors, counselors, classes, books, the Internet, or any resource that will teach you how to accomplish your goals. In minutes, I showed Patti how to compute a discount on a pocket calculator, and most of her math fear disappeared.

3. **Improve your self-esteem.** You can feel more competent and confident in the following way. Catch yourself thinking self-disparaging thoughts and either dispute them or detach emotionally. Patti's core belief was, "I'm not smart enough to work with the public." Her disputation was: "I'm smart enough to know the name of nearly every plant in *The New Western Garden Book*, so I'm smart enough to help people find what they want." When Patti

had thoughts like, *I'll freeze up*, or *They'll fire me when they realize I'm an imposter*, she detached by reminding herself, "That's just a thought. I don't have to buy into it."

4. **Set effective goals.** To crystallize your goal, write it down as a positive statement. With Patti, this meant, "Stand up to fear and get a job," rather than "Don't give in to your stupid fears." Once you've set a realistic goal in writing, identify obstacles and deal with them. For Patti, the only real obstacle was her lack of confidence, so we traced the origin of this issue to believing her parents' definition of her. From there, we worked on Patti redeciding that their negative messages were projections of their own inadequacies and not really about her. This led to a new and heartfelt acceptance of herself as both good and competent.

5. **Practice positive self-talk.** Positive self-talk is based on self-awareness, reality, and achievement. Notice when your inner voice is negative. Remember, negativity is just a home movie. You can also play a different movie—a positive one! Patti used her inner voice to cheer herself on and support her ambitions. Examples of her self-talk include: "I can do this!" "Go for it!" "Good job!"

6. **Listen to your inner skeptic.** Your inner skeptic is the discerning part of you that knows when you need to look further into something before taking the leap. Don't confuse your inner skeptic with negative self-talk. The latter leaves you feeling diminished or inadequate, whereas your skeptic is intuitive and keeps you grounded in reality. It may tell you you're not ready to quit your job or launch that new software company.

7. **Identify your fears.** Fears cannot be worked through without being faced. You can't get over your fear of elevators by taking the stairs! Is there a real danger connected with your fear? If so, deal with it by putting it on your "to-do" list and taking the appropriate action.

Such a list will prepare you to achieve goals by addressing the fears that stop you. Patti had to work directly with people to show herself she could get past the anxiety that plagued her (see chapter 33, "Fear Is No Burden).

8. **Build a balanced life.** Find a healthy balance for your many lives—social, work, family, friends, spiritual, and community. Build a support system that includes safe persons around you, and share your dreams. You already "have a life," so use it skillfully while you work toward your goals.

9. **Take small steps.** We walk before we run. Take "baby steps" en route to your goal. Consider what happens when we take too big a step. We feel overwhelmed, become immobilized, and procrastinate. The ancient Tao Te Ching teaches us to "…accomplish the great task by a series of small acts." One of Patti's homework assignments was to compile a list of every nursery within fifteen miles of her home. There was no expectation to put in an application, merely make the list.

10. **Pace yourself.** Tell yourself that accomplishing your goal is a marathon, not a sprint. It takes time to work the steps, so make the decision to tend your own garden and not everyone else's. Expect the unexpected, and adjust your steps accordingly. You may need to give something up in order to take something else on.

11. **Don't burn out.** You will accomplish more if you take good care of yourself. No one can do it for you. Build in an early warning system to detect stress cues, such as headaches, muscular tension, stomach problems and irritability, lack of energy, or depression. If you are still unable to make healthy choices, get immediate professional help.

12. **Let go of perfectionism.** Perfectionism will decommission the process of moving toward your goal. Give it your "best effort" instead of trying to do things perfectly. It is an illusion to believe that you can do things perfectly, one that sets you up for disappointment and a sense of failure. Accept the fact you will make a few mistakes along the way. Learn from them, and let them go. Please see chapter 53, "The Curse of Perfectionism" as there are certain times when you need to know you've given it your best shot in order to let go.

Follow these suggestions and enhance your potential for success. In many families, this information is neither verbally taught nor modeled through constructive action. Patti's family of origin never prepared her to face the world and, in fact, undermined her sense of self by making her feel incompetent and stupid. It is no wonder she lacked the confidence to even try.

On a brilliant spring day several years ago, a close friend asked Patti to accompany her to a local nursery to help her choose some blueberry plants. She wanted varieties that would produce an early, midseason, and late crop of berries, and she knew Patti would know the right ones to purchase. In the checkout line, the friend pointed out a sign that read, "Now Hiring." With a little urging, Patti put in an application and was hired several days later. Within a year, she became their "go-to" information expert in the outdoor garden section, answering questions on every aspect of home gardening. She has also won awards for her magnificent planter designs at major home shows. By working hard to put the suggestions into practice, Patti achieved her goals and changed her life.

Until one is committed, there is hesitancy, the chance to draw back. Concerning all acts of initiative (and creation), there is one elementary truth, the ignorance of which kills countless ideas and splendid plans: that the moment one definitely commits oneself, then Providence moves too. All sorts of things occur to help one that would never otherwise have occurred. A whole stream of events issues from the decision, raising in one's favor all manner of unforeseen incidents and meetings and material assistance, which no man could have dreamed would have come his way.

—W. H. Murray

Whatever you can do, or dream you can do, begin it. Boldness has genius, power, and magic in it. Begin it now.

—Goethe

Achieving Goals—The Art of Calculated Risk Worksheet

1. **What are your dreams?** (Live in a foreign country, start a new business…)

_____

_____

_____

2. **What skills…**

Do you have?	Do you need?	Where can you develop them?
EX. Good communicator and organizer	Speak foreign language	College class, a language institute, find a friend to practice with, CDs
_____	_____	_____
_____	_____	_____
_____	_____	_____
_____	_____	_____
_____	_____	_____

3. **Take steps to improve your confidence.**

   a. **What negative self-talk can you change to improve self-esteem?** ("I can't make my goals happen. I'm not brave enough.")

   _____

   _____

   _____

   b. How can you dispute the negative self-talk? ("I'm brave enough. I can accomplish it.")

   _____

   _____

   _____

4. Set achievable goals based on reality. (Affordable housing, job openings)

   _____

   _____

   _____

5. Practice positive self-talk. List positive messages that you need to tell yourself. ("I can accomplish anything I set my mind to." "I can learn to do the things that I don't know how to do."):

   _____

   _____

   _____

6. What is your inner skeptic saying? ("Living in a foreign country will end my friendships—I can find a way to stay in touch." "This is a politically unstable country; my safety may be compromised—I will take a closer look at this.")

   _____

   _____

   _____

7. Address your fears.

   a. Identify your fears. (Worry about keeping friendships.)

   _____

   _____

   _____

b. **What can you do to work on them?** (Talk to friends about concerns, make a plan to keep in touch.)

_____

_____

_____

8. **Build a balanced life.** (Cut back on work hours, develop a stronger support system with friends.)

_____

_____

_____

9. **Break your goals into small, manageable steps.** (Goal: Find a job abroad. Steps: 1. research job market in the countries of interest, 2. pick jobs of interest to apply to, 3. prepare or find someone to help with résumé, 4. submit résumé…)

_____

_____

_____

10. **Pace yourself.** Set a realistic time line for completion of your goals. (Five months to find job: 1. three months to research job market, 2. one month to pick jobs of interest 3. two weeks to prepare résumés, 4. two weeks to submit résumés…)

_____

_____

_____

11. **Don't burn out.** List your stress cues (headache, stomach problems, exhaustion, sleeplessness):

_____

_____

_____

12.Let go of perfectionism. Develop self-talk for giving it your best effort.
("I'm going to make mistakes along the way, and I will learn from them.")

_____

_____

_____

Success is the sum of small efforts—repeated day in and day out.
—Robert Collier

Goals are dreams we convert to plans and take action to fulfill.
—Zig Ziglar

52
Decision-Making 1 + 2 = 3

Once you make a decision, the universe conspires to make it happen.
—Ralph Waldo Emerson

Accept no one's definition of your life, but define yourself.
—Fierstein Harvey

Chocolate or vanilla? In or out? Paper or plastic? Pass or punt? Yes or no? Buy or sell? Decisions shape our destinies, and yet in today's modern world, we often don't have the time to think things through. Sometimes we decide quickly and unconsciously; sometimes we agonize forever and still can't decide.

This much I know. In order to cope successfully, we must make good decisions and stick by them. If we are to be happy with ourselves and the lives we create, we must have an effective decision-making strategy in our toolbox for life.

Consider the following scenarios and the possible consequences of making the "wrong" choice.

- Should I buy the chocolate cheesecake ice cream or some fresh fruit?
- Should I take that job and move away from my family or stay put?
- What would be a great Valentine's gift for my new partner?
- Should I accept Kevin's proposal of marriage?
- Should I ask for help with my depression or lick my own wounds?

Obviously, the stakes are high when we make important life decisions. It's not such a big deal if we choose the wrong Valentine's Day gift, but choosing the wrong husband could be a disaster on every front. Happiness demands that we enter into the decision-making process with awareness, skill, and inner wisdom. If we lack any one of those ingredients, we set ourselves up for disappointment and self-blame. No wonder many of us dread making difficult decisions and end up confused, stuck in procrastination, and paralyzed over the fear we will not choose wisely.

I have found the "Wise Mind" concept can be quite useful in making good decisions, both in my personal life and psychotherapy practice. This idea comes from Dialectical Behavior Therapy (DBT), a form of psychotherapy developed by Dr. Marsha Linehan at the University of Washington. DBT is a research-proven approach that integrates Western cognitive-behavioral techniques with Buddhist meditation practices to bring about emotional self-regulation and mindfulness. It is considered the treatment of choice for persons with unstable moods and chaotic interpersonal relationships. Let's be honest. Aren't we all a little like that from time to time?

Every woman has a Wise Mind, but all too few put it to use, especially when our feelings are running "hot." To put your Wise Mind into action, you must differentiate between your emotional mind and your reasonable mind. The emotional mind tends to be intense and reactive and often leads to impulsive and careless decision-making. The emotional mind isn't a bad thing because emotions serve a purpose. We just don't want to be ruled solely by emotion.

The reasonable mind is about being factual, logical, and rational. If you're following a difficult recipe, solving a Sudoku puzzle, or laying out a detailed project time line at work, you are relying on the reasonable mind. Similarly, we don't want to be ruled only by our reasonable minds, lest we end up some feminine version of "Spock" (the overly logical and cerebral Vulcan science officer on the Star Trek series, who, interestingly, was the counterpart to the overly emotional medical officer "Bones" McCoy). The optimal ideal would be to be part Spock, part McCoy.

The Wise Mind thus represents an integration of the emotional mind and reasonable mind and becomes the key to making better decisions.

Consider the following example. "I *really* want that flashy new car with leather seats and its new car smell (emotional mind), but I'll have to take on an enormous monthly payment to get it" (reasonable mind). "I think I'll fix the transmission in my old car for now and start a separate savings account for a new one" (Wise Mind).

When we're able to integrate information that is both emotionally charged and tempered by reason, decisions feel good, intuitive. A Wise Mind decision gives us a felt sense in the body, often the belly or the heart, telling us we are on the right track. There is less anxiety or confusion because decisions that connect emotion and reason feel true or right. We get an afterglow, not an afterburn.

Molly, a normally shy and quiet college student, had been in treatment with me for half a year to get over social anxiety. After phoning for an urgent after-hours appointment, she arrived in my waiting room in obvious emotional distress. Before we made it into my office, she blurted out, "I've made a terrible mistake."

She proceeded to tell me about a friend's Halloween party where she downed "more than ten" tequila-spiked Jell-O shots. Molly confessed that she used alcohol and occasionally marijuana in order to "loosen up" and enjoy herself in social situations (unfortunately, this is also an effective way to disconnect your reasonable mind). Toward the end of the evening, a classmate she barely knew began flirting with her, and they ended up having sex on her friend's bed. The young man was at least responsible enough to use a condom, but also under the influence, he put it on inside out and it came off inside Molly.

To make matters worse, just before our session, Molly had tested positive on a home pregnancy test. Her head rang so loudly with the anticipated judgments of her friends and family, she could barely hear herself think. I asked Molly to take some deep-down-through-her-body breaths and recall a time when she felt calm and together. In a few minutes, after sharing a memory of being held and comforted by her loving grandmother, she settled down enough to discuss her circumstances.

Now able to center herself, Molly and I together posed a number of relevant questions that would dominate her thinking over the next month.

"Who is safe enough that I could share my dilemma? Given my struggle with social anxiety, how would I cope with the embarrassment of being pregnant and unmarried or raising a child as a single mother? Would I be up to the physical changes associated with pregnancy and the inconvenience and pain of childbirth? Do I have the financial wherewithal to raise this child and afford her or him the necessities of a good childhood? Should I get an abortion or carry this pregnancy to term? Would a future mate reject me if I was raising a child born out of wedlock or if I'd given up an infant for adoption? If I become a mother, should I give up my education and raise the child or adopt it out to a family who can't have their own children? How should I involve the child's father in deciding?"

Talk about crucial life decisions! How does one go about the process of deciding when there is so much on the line, so many positives and negatives? Here is the three-step sequential method I used with Molly.

Step 1: What is the Issue?

a. **Gather emotional data.** The purpose here is to consciously assess your emotional mind. *How am I feeling as a result of this issue? What feelings, regardless of how unpleasant, need to be accepted? Am I tuning in to my own inner voice or inner guide? Could I be caving in to peer pressure or 'group think'? What do I want for myself in making this decision?* Observe any emotions that might be reactions to the approaching decision, e.g., anxiety, guilt, shame, dread, regret, relief, happiness, and anticipated pleasure. Be honest and curious about all your feelings. Journal them. They are arrows to direct you toward the right decision. They will help you find your path.

b. **Gather reasonable data about the issue.** Now we plug into the reasonable mind. We do the emotional mind first because emotions usually come online first, so we go with the freshest fish. Ask yourself: *Just what exactly is the problem? What do I need to know, and where do I gather that information? What are the consequences of each possible choice? Could I be screening out important information because of selective percep-*

tion? With whom do I consult? What is the easiest, most effective way to get the information I need (counselor, pastor, family, friends, mentors, Internet, seminars, reading, tapes, journals, and so on)? What other factors need consideration?

c. **Ask, "What are my fears?"** Some type of fear typically pops up as we contemplate important decisions. Ask yourself, *What is my worst fear?* If your fears are realistic, address them head-on. If not, have a chuckle and let them go. If you are "hooked" by anxiety-provoking thoughts, watch your self-talk and detach. For example, instead of Molly saying to herself, *If I carry to term, the baby will likely have a birth defect because of how he or she was conceived,* she could say, *My mind is imagining catastrophes and frightening me. I can consult with my physician and see if prenatal testing is even necessary.* Please see chapter 33, "Fear Is No Burden."

Step 2: Do the Balancing Test.

a. **List the pros and cons**. Writing out the advantages and disadvantages of each option is a technique advocated by both the philosopher Plato and Benjamin Franklin (not bad company for anyone to keep). *How will each side of a particular decision affect me? How will it affect important others? What are the potential long- and short-term impacts? What are my most important concerns? What risks are there on each side of the decision? How much is it likely to cost me if I'm wrong?*

b. **Create new alternatives.** Think outside the box. Brainstorm the possible choices. Don't accept the first alternative just because it looks like it might work. Challenge any limits you've put on your thinking about the decision. Visit your library of past experiences to see if there's something as yet unexplored to draw upon. Brainstorm with someone older and more experienced. Ask a wise and trusted other for any suggestions or practical advice.

Step 3: Make the Decision: 1 + 2 = 3.

a. **If you're stuck, ask yourself,** *Am I telling myself something that is making me feel stuck? Is there pertinent information I've not yet gathered?* If there is, go get it. Check your body and mind for fears you've either not identified or not yet fully addressed. Contemplate what you're trying to gain from making this decision. Access your Wise Mind. Consult your intuition and gut instincts. Meditate to open what is closed in you and balance what is reactive. Journal your dreams for clues. Pray for guidance.

b. **Have backup plans.** Pay attention as you execute your plan. Be open to the possibility that your first decision might not be the best one or right one. Consider alternative courses of action. If you simply don't fit at the college you chose because it's just too big and impersonal, start looking for a smaller one and transfer. If you choose to move to Phoenix but are unsure whether you can deal with 110-degree days, you must have a backup plan to move to a cooler clime.

c. **Take the action steps necessary to carry out the decision.** Figure out what has to be done to put your ultimate decision into action. Is it on hold until some condition is met, such as finding out where you stand (e.g., "I'll take that job if they'll give me fifty thousand a year and full benefits")? Write out a time line for the various steps you must take. Who must be told? What arrangements must be in place? What resources will you need to give your choice every chance of working?

After carefully working through the steps, Molly ultimately made her decision based on clarifying her own value system, which honored all life. Wise Mind told her she would always regret an abortion, and she felt a sense of relief when she made her final choice. Her pros and cons list was heavily weighted toward carrying the child to term and taking on the parent role. She never did achieve an absolute sense of certainty but accepted that whatever choice she made would come with some degree of self-doubt. In consulting family, friends, Planned Parenthood, and the father of the child, Molly received a great deal of contradictory opinions.

I stayed away from offering my view of what I thought best for her, as would most mental health professionals. It was her decision, and she made it after considering input from both the emotional mind and reasonable mind. In the end, she had a good feeling about her decision. I am proud of Molly, and I admire her courage and heart. She is currently raising a healthy, adorable one-year-old girl and attending a local community college part-time.

$1 + 2 = 3$.

How to Make a Decision Worksheet

Step 1. What is the Issue?

_____

_____

_____

    a) Emotional Data:

       _____

       _____

       _____

       _____

    b) Reasonable Data:

       _____

       _____

       _____

       _____

    c) Fears/Attending to Them:

       _____

       _____

       _____

       _____

Step 2. Balancing Test.

Pros: _____   *Cons:* _____
       _____   _____
       _____   _____
       _____   _____
       _____   _____
       _____   _____
       _____   _____
       _____   _____
       _____   _____
       _____   _____
       _____   _____
       _____   _____
       _____   _____

Create new alternatives:

_____
_____
_____

Step 3. The Decision is Step 1 + Step 2.

1. Decision:

_____
_____
_____
_____
_____
_____

2. Backup Plan(s):

_____

_____

_____

_____

_____

_____

3. Action Steps:

1. _____

_____

2. _____

_____

3. _____

_____

4. _____

_____

5. _____

_____

53
The Curse of Perfectionism

Aim for success, not perfection. Never give up your right to be wrong, because then you will lose the ability to learn new things and move forward with your life.

—David Burns

Remember that fear always lurks behind perfectionism. Confronting your fears and allowing yourself the right to be human can, paradoxically, make you a far happier and more productive person.

—David Burns

Perfectionism is a curse that dooms the perfectionist to further failures and an even greater sense of inadequacy. It is a set-up to fail because no one will ever attain perfection.

—Stanley Wilson

Perfectionists often suffer from anxiety, frustration, depression, shame, or obsessiveness—sometimes, all of the above. They are plagued by low self-esteem and actually may produce less as a result of their impossible ideals. Most have troubled relationships, as their self-talk is negative and their conversations with others are irritable and disconnected. Because they strive for perfection themselves, they project onto others and perceive others as critical even when they're not. Some people believe that perfectionism drives them to levels of excellence and productivity that they never could obtain otherwise. This belief is popular. We hear athletes and coaches glorify the phrase "no pain, no gain!"

Perfectionists perceive themselves as inefficient because they imagine successful people achieve personal goals with little effort, few errors, maximum self-confidence, and minimal emotional distress. Not surprisingly, they are likely to view their efforts to cope as inadequate, even when the truth is they're doing fine. Negative self-talk can profoundly slow down, shut down, or cause perfectionists to operate under extreme pressure. Dwelling on their shortcomings, they judge themselves as unrewarded and inferior. This, in turn, robs them of satisfaction, maintains their low self-esteem, and further undermines their motivation.

Perfectionism is a state of mind that tears at our self-worth. It's a setup to feel bad about yourself. No one can do things perfectly unless you are God or a deity. Since perfection is unattainable, failure to achieve it is inevitable and helplessness sets in. Next comes procrastination and paralysis, high anxiety and episodes of depression. All we can do is operate from our integrity, which means doing the best job we can given our circumstances, time, resources, money, focus, and energy.

A former client comes to mind. Kayla, a middle-aged woman, is a talented landscaper operating her own business. Her problem is she tries to do a perfect job every time, and she came to treatment after realizing this attitude is causing her chronic anxiety, low self-esteem, and physical and mental exhaustion. She constantly worries about what her customers expect and what constitutes perfection. Is the rhododendron planted in the optimal place given its sun requirements? Should I move it six inches to the east? Did I put in enough lawn to give their children a nice play area? Maybe a few more square feet or maybe not? Is the new tree rotated properly to afford the best possible view from the patio? Or should it view best from the kitchen window? Have I properly barked the planting areas to keep down the weeds? Should I have put down weedkiller? Is it bad to use weedkiller given environmental concerns? Do I have just the right color flowers in the area seen from their bay window? Should I plant annuals or perennials? Is the ground going to hold the moisture sufficiently to support the blueberries on the side of the house? Too dry? Too soggy? What if they would bear more fruit up on the hill? Are the stones on the path the perfect distance for optimal walking? And so on, ad nauseam.

Kayla questions if she can continue with her career if she can't let go of perfectionism—and rightly so. We explored how she got to be this way and learned she had to be perfect or risk censure and shame from both parents. She was not allowed to make mistakes, and striving for perfection as an adult was an unconscious attempt to compensate for a self that felt fundamentally flawed, undeserving, and unlovable. If she got the job perfectly, Kayla reasoned (below the surface), she would show that she was worthy and competent. After working at the core of believing that her worth was not contingent on doing things perfectly, we agreed upon the value of doing things well. Kayla experimented with giving it her best shot and realizing on every job that there would be flaws and even mistakes.

Kayla's real job was to give it her best effort without making herself crazy. She was instructed to stand back, observe her work objectively, and if there was nothing standing out that needed correction (a shrub left untrimmed, weeds taking over a planting area, and so on), to walk away. She could then say, "I've done the best I can given the time constraints and what I have to work with. Nothing is perfect, including me." Kayla not only kept her job but reported that her productivity and profitability increased almost twofold!

Here are some useful questions to ask yourself when confronting the curse:

- How much time should I spend on this?
- Can I accept the fact that I will never be perfect and let go of the striving?
- Is my self-worth contingent on doing this perfectly?
- What is important to do on this job?
- How far should I go?
- Can I accept criticism without going into self-loathing and despair?
- Can I catch myself automatically criticizing my performance and stop doing it?
- What is expected of me on this job?
- If I don't know what is expected of me, can I get it clarified?
- What will I or they be satisfied with?

- What would it be like to surrender to my own humanness and accept my flaws?
- Am I less of a person if I make a mistake here?
- Can I step away so that I won't obsess or overwork it?
- What's the main focus of this job?
- Is it possible the mistake I just made is an opportunity for growth or learning?
- How will I feel if I overdo the job?
- Am I finally able to forgive the mistakes I've made and move on?
- Can I operate from my Adult, give it my best, and let go?
- Can I love the Child in me who took so much criticism for making mistakes?
- If I feel myself tensing over my perfectionism, can I relax my heart and let it go?
- If my "old story" is I have to be perfect, can I author a "new story" for myself?

The best treatment for perfectionism is thought reform (please see chapter 21, "Reframing"). Thought reform is the antidote to the perfectionist ideal; that is, you reform your thoughts to accept the essential pain that you're never going to be perfect, to accept your imperfections as evidence of your humanness, and to know you are lovable even if you're flawed…and that it's all OK.

I will hold myself to a standard of grace not perfection.

—Emily Ley

54
Handling Stress on the Job

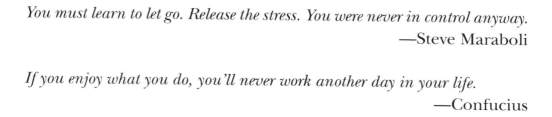

You must learn to let go. Release the stress. You were never in control anyway.
—Steve Maraboli

If you enjoy what you do, you'll never work another day in your life.
—Confucius

Let's keep it simple and define stress as the experience of physical and emotional tension that happens when we face demanding situations. Stress is our built-in way of responding to a stimulus, a challenge from the environment. Sometimes stress mobilizes us in a way to cope at our highest potentials, and sometimes, it becomes too much to bear. When the latter happens, stress may overtake our coping abilities and leave us feeling overwhelmed and suffering from physical symptoms that range from a sour stomach to a chronic illness.

Given enough stress, our body will go into the "fight-or-flight response." This means our body will produce cortisol and adrenaline, causing a rise in blood pressure, rapid breathing, higher heart rate, tense muscles, and extra alertness. This is good and has survival value if we're hiking in the woods and find ourselves confronted by a grizzly bear, but it's not so good if it becomes a chronic way of reacting to more mundane situations.

For instance, imagine you are at work and the boss stops by to tell you there's been a change in priorities and a deadline that was set for the end of the month has been moved up by two weeks. Yes, this is stressful, but it is a challenge that should get you going in a positive way. If you use it as motivation, you can step up your pace and meet the boss's new deadline. However, if you overreact, as if there is a real danger present, and go into "fight-or-flight" mode, you are likely to develop some unwanted physical and emotional symptoms.

Pamela is a successful middle-aged manager who earns a six-figure income at a major corporation. Her bosses work the heck out of her, expect her to put in overtime without pay, assign her deadlines no one could possibly meet, give her a lot of responsibility but little power, ask her to take on certain tasks and then contradict themselves, and create a hostile work environment by unfairly criticizing her performance. Not surprisingly, Pamela's health has suffered from the stress of her work circumstances; in other words, her body has kept score. She developed migraines, back and neck aches, crippling fatigue, and depression.

While Pamela's situation may seem a dramatic example, it is all too common for those who face too much stress at work. The following is a list of common job-related stress symptoms:

- **Physical symptoms:** high blood pressure; heart palpitations; insomnia; hypersomnia; constant fatigue; headaches; backaches; skin rashes; digestive disorders; ulcers; colitis; loss of appetite; overeating; nausea; breathlessness or a dry mouth; and numbness in the arms, hands, or feet. Obviously, some of these symptoms are serious, or could be if untreated. Check with your doctor to rule out potentially significant problems.

- **Emotional symptoms:** depression, cynicism, and feelings of helplessness or failure; anxiety, chronic worry, panic disorder, or becoming overemotional or aggressive in conflict situations; loss of interest in personal appearance, distancing from other people, social events, or previously enjoyed activities; poor concentration, difficulty remembering or making decisions; sadness, guilt, fatigue, apathy, impulsiveness, or poor judgment; loss of confidence in personal ability; and lack of self-worth.

- **Spiritual symptoms:** Distancing from spiritual connections; not praying; not attending church; or not meditating.

Think of these symptoms, especially the more minor ones, as warning flags that spur you to action. To cope with stress on the job, it is important to devote some time every day to one or more of the following strategies. I suggest for most people twenty minutes in the morning and twenty minutes in the late afternoon or early evening. Taking into account the rules in your workplace as well as safety considerations, here are some practical ideas that are useful to deal with stress on the job. Much of this is common sense, and I apologize in advance if you already know it:

1. **Environmental**
   - Play relaxing or uplifting music, and try noise-reducing headphones or earbuds for more quiet and privacy.
   - Bring in pets that can be low-maintenance buddies (unless your workplace is especially pet-friendly, it's best to leave cats, dogs, and birds at home).
   - Have easy-to-maintain plants.
   - Hang signs or objects with positive sayings.
   - Surround yourself with lighting that is warm, not fluorescent; if you can get a window, great!
   - Display pictures of family, friends, relaxing scenes, trips, animals, favorite activities, or humorous scenes.
   - Use ergonomically designed and supportive chairs for proper back and leg care. A rocker is great, and so are footstools.
   - Take breaks from using the computer or desk and stretch. Move around, and get your blood flowing. Better yet, stand and work if you can. This, according to research, is even more important for women than men.
   - Reclaim your desk or workspace and get organized. Simplify, prioritize, and eliminate unnecessary paperwork.
   - Play with toys you can manipulate with your hands, like squeeze balls, marbles, rocks, or a Nerf basketball and hoop.
   - Find a comfortable temperature to work in. Bring a sweater and dress in layers if the environment is uncontrollable or unpredictable.

- Lower the noise level with soundproofing or putting material on the walls or door. Sound machines that produce white noise or noise-cancelling earphones can help.
- Eliminate fumes from the area if possible, using an open window or air filters. Fumes can cause mood swings, irritability, headaches, skin disorders, immune system compromise, and so on.
- Have a bulletin board for jokes, quotes, thoughtful reflections, communications, and upcoming events.

2. Foods
- Keep healthy foods for regular snacks nearby—fruit, veggies, nuts, decaffeinated coffee or herbal tea, for example. Eat regularly three meals a day and low-carbohydrate snacks in between. Consider lowering your gluten intake.
- Limit your caffeine and sugar intake. Stay away from them or maintain a low level.
- Avoid excessive alcohol consumption.

3. Exercise
- Have a regular program (three or four times a week for not less than one-half hour), whatever fits your interest and style.
- Get a massage or do Yoga, Tai Chi, or Qi Gong, and so on. You might be able to do this on your lunch hour.
- At a minimum, go for walk around the block while on the job and stretch standing up or sitting down during a break. Call friends or loved ones while on a lunch break, especially if you need to connect with someone for support.
- If you can bring your dog, take it for walks.

4. People and Coworkers
- Ask yourself if people you work with contribute to your tension. Can they problem-solve, or do they add to the problems with

gossip and other such behaviors? Avoid the ones who do, unless you have to engage with them to complete work tasks.

- Don't share personal issues with coworkers, unless they are close friends and you are 100 percent certain you can speak in confidence.
- Minimize contact with toxic coworkers. Be courteous and professional, but minimize discussions and interactions with such persons.
- Stick strictly to business at work. Don't be on Facebook, Twitter, or other social media sites where you can set yourself up for a reprimand.
- Don't date coworkers, or do so at your own peril. It is generally good policy to follow the old adage: "Don't fish off the company pier!"

5. Personal

- Practice slow, deep breathing in to the count of four, hold for four, and out for four. Slowly build your number until you can get to twelve.
- Try hypnosis or stress-reduction CDs for relaxation while on breaks.
- Visualize a beautiful, relaxing scene or place you have been or want to visit.
- Join a group of business owners or industry professionals, and brainstorm problems or share information.
- Attend classes or seminars for making business more efficient.
- Keep the right *balance* between work, family, and play.
- Use positive self-talk and catch yourself when you're doing otherwise.
- Pray regularly, if so inclined. If not, meditate.
- Read a good book on your break.
- Do not use street drugs that may lead to addiction.
- Be wary of prescription drugs that foster addiction.

6. Time Planning

- Take regular breaks during the day; take care of yourself (mind, body, and spirit).
- Take time off, especially when you know you need it. Stagger days off with your spouse (if you want alone time) and people you work with.
- Use caller ID to screen your calls for work.
- Take regular planned vacations. Don't wait until the stress is unbearable, your family complains, or your health is affected.
- Take sick days when you are sick; that's why we have them. Use the time to nurture yourself and recover.

7. Setting Limits

- Get a good idea of what you can do in your business day/ week without it affecting your physical or emotional health and without having an adverse effect on your family life.
- Know your limits. Don't try to be Superwoman or Superman.
- Weigh what is most important: demands of work, need to make money, or taking time off. Strike the proper balance.
- Learn to skillfully say "no" to overtime or extra projects that go beyond your job description or compromise your health.
- Post signs, shut your door, and advise people when you are available and when you're not so you can work more effectively and have necessary quiet time.

8. Delegating

- Keep your workload at a manageable level. Be honest with yourself and others regarding your capacities.
- Delegate projects to others, if at all possible, before you are overwhelmed.
- To prevent burnout, delegate if you are given too much responsibility or too little power.

9. Dealing with Dissatisfaction

- Request to be reassigned to different tasks or varying tasks.
- Request to be reassigned to a different department.
- Communicate clearly your concerns to the appropriate manager or administrator. Follow it up with problem-solving solutions.
- If you have a Human Resources Department, tactfully explore whether they are, in fact, there to serve you or if they are more pro-company. If they really work for the employees, use them as a resource. At the risk of offending someone, I have seen too many HR requests for help backfire.

10. Reassessing Your Purpose and Goals

- Get clear as to what your purpose is at work.
- Reevaluate and set new goals—both short- and long-term.
- Attend seminars and training that will energize your goals and purpose or to find a new job.
- Don't be afraid to look for another job if yours is too stressful, but do it with care and tact so as not to defeat your intentions.

These ideas are good medicine culled from forty years of work. If you've taken the "medicine" and are still having problems, seek help from a counselor, naturopath, medical doctor, minister, career coach, or friends; look for a new job or reevaluate why you are still with this job. If economic issues force you to stay on the job, practice the listed suggestions as much as possible and surround yourself with a positive support system until you can make a change. You can't eliminate stress on the job, but you can cope with it effectively.

One Step at a Time

Rows of ragged rocks outline a path for healing?

Brown, decaying leaves hug the winter ground—a blanket to transform?

The labyrinth awaits the sojourner—
almost calls her name—
Will you enter my simple boundaries
and journey my paths
One Step at a Time?

Straight ahead, yet winding and crooked
The curled road beckons to be trod—
reinforcing the uplifted
blessing the downtrodden
Maybe tears, maybe joy, maybe peace
One Step at a Time.

All who are heavy laden, come stand at the gate
All who are fragmented, place one foot down
and the other in front
All who find wonder in the commonplace,
Come travel the narrow rows
One Step at a Time.

Give up your burdens, your middle of the night worries
Lay a care on a silver, craggly rock as you pass
and move on to the next,
the monotony will soothe you
One Step at a Time.

Moving inward,
The trail winds in and out
Muscles untensing,

The walker's job seems easy,
The cares tumble down
and hit the ground with imagined force
lightening the load on contact
One Step at a Time.

Step 48, step 49, many more follow
while curling toward center like a
snail into its shell
Motionless at last,
a wooden cross is sighted,
God's presence overwhelms
and envelopes the inner sanctum—
His peace now a cloister
on the journey half over
One Step at a Time.

The pause to discover
new perspectives to ponder
fresh eyes, lightened heart
the world is a wonder
with steps unencumbered
the pilgrimage rewinds
One Step at a Time.

The breathing is slower
the feet touch down lower,
and easier on the road well-worn
The unknown, now familiar
the end is the beginning
the sad is now glory
All happening unexpectedly
One Step at a Time.

A twist inward
A transformation outward
A fresh view from fatigued eyes
All part of a simple design
of much complexity
with the whole greater
than the sum of the steps
All the while traveling
One Step at a Time.

—Suzanne Moody

About the Author

Diana F. Lee is an accomplished counselor with four decades of experience empowering people to resolve issues and make positive changes. She emphasizes skill building, grief work, and creativity while collaborating with other health-care professionals to facilitate improved self-esteem and a balanced, spiritually-based lifestyle.

She was born and raised in the Pacific Northwest and spent twenty-six years as a resident of Snohomish, Washington. She loves nature and, until recently, lived on a small farm that was a home for horses, goats, geese, ducks, dogs, and cats. She and her attorney husband of forty years, William, have recently moved to the "art town" of La Conner, Washington. They have a daughter, Katherine, who is also an attorney.

Diana has master's degrees in Education/Counseling and Public Administration, and a post-master's certificate in Transforming Spirituality, all from Seattle University. She worked as a probation officer for fifteen years and has been in private practice since 1983 treating individuals, families, and couples. For the last fourteen years, she has used three Brussels Griffon as therapy dogs in her practice.

She has also completed a program in counseling chemical dependency issues and has done many years of group work with adults in addiction recovery. She is currently working as a Spiritual Director in her private practice as well. She is a local and international (Russia and China) speaker on mental health and addiction issues.

Diana is the author of *Rustproof Relationships: A Guide to Healthy Relationships and Effective Coping Skills*, *Touching the Soul (a therapeutic guide to spiritual and personal growth)*, and *Therapy Dogs and the Stories They Can Tell*. She is currently working on her fifth book *Horses: Resilience ad Renewal*.

Diana loves to travel and has been profoundly influenced by European, Asian, and Russian cultures. With her interest in spiritual growth, Diana has visited numerous temples, churches, monasteries, and other sacred sites. A lifelong lover of horses, she has ridden in most of the countries she has visited. She has many creative outlets and has held numerous art shows that included wall hangings, photography, clothing, purses, and jewelry. She also enjoys designing gardens and homes.

About the Dogs

Dr. Jerry, Jerome Samuel Taylor, was a great boy who worked at the office since he was one year of age. He passed away in 2016 at the age of fourteen. He loved to go to the waiting room and greet the clients. He was known to lick the tears off of the cheeks of clients if they wished. He quite often got out of his bed and would go over to clients, sit by them, and put a paw on their lap or arm to comfort them. Dr. Jerry was helpful to patients with Post Traumatic Stress Disorder and Depression. He always knew when the sessions were finished and waited quietly by the door to say good-bye.

Jack McCoy Taylor is the rebel. He is a boundary violator. Jack loves people and wants to be in their faces. I bring him to work when I have clients who are rebellious. I tell them he is a rebel and perhaps they can relate to him. I once had a client who told his story after Jack rolled over belly-up on his lap. The client said, "If he can show the underside of his belly, then so can I." He proceeded to tell his story. Jack also responds well to the phrase, "Where are your boundaries?" He backs up, sits down, and waits patiently. Clients love it, and it makes them laugh. I use him with clients to practice setting boundaries firmly without apologizing or feeling bad. They get lots of practice.

Jenny Taylor passed away in December 2010. She had a gift for treating people who had been abused and molested. She would climb up on clients' laps and put a paw on them when they cried, told their story, or did Guided Imagery work. She had a way of looking into clients' eyes as if to say, "I care about you and know your pain." She was fourteen years old when she passed.

These three courageous, loving Brussels Griffons have provided wonderful, empathetic responses to clients in my workplace. It is important to acknowledge their accomplishments because they have created a special, nurturing, safe place for the clients to work. I love them dearly, and so do my clients.

There is a mountain of research on the effectiveness and benefits of animal-assisted therapy, for example, reduced anxiety and depression, reduced loneliness, lower stress levels, and improved overall health.

CPSIA information can be obtained
at www.ICGtesting.com
Printed in the USA
BVHW010915091219
566077BV00007B/125/P

9 781466 454927